HOME OFFICE

The Sentence of the Court

A Handbook for Courts
on the Treatment
of Offenders

LONDON

HMSO

ISBN 0 11 340985 0

Foreword by the Home Secretary

This booklet aims to provide judges and magistrates with a concise guide to the sentencing powers available to them under the present law, and the basic principles applicable to their use.

The first edition of 'The Sentence of the Court' was published in 1964, following a recommendation by the Streatfeild committee that sentencers should be supplied with general information about the content and effect of the various sentences at their disposal.

The last edition appeared in 1986. There have been many changes in criminal justice legislation since that time, and the Criminal Justice Act 1988, in particular, has made it necessary to revise and update the text. This new edition has now been prepared with the support of the Judicial Studies Board. The Chairman, Lord Justice Glidewell, and I are pleased to commend it to sentencers. We hope that they, and the many others who are concerned with the administration of criminal justice, will continue to find this handbook a valuable guide to sentencing.

Contents

CHAPTER 1

Introduction

1.1 This book considers in turn the basic principles of sentencing offenders and the context in which it takes place; the basic penalties available to the courts; the special problems of dealing with certain kinds of offender and, finally, some of the more important ancillary orders which the courts may make in appropriate cases in addition to imposing one of the basic penalties. The following paragraphs briefly outline these sections of the text in turn.

1.2 *Chapter 2* is concerned with the courts themselves: their heirarchy and the interaction between them. *Chapter 3* considers basic questions common to all sentencing decisions: paragraphs 3.2–3.13 discuss the aims of sentencing and the choice of sentence; paragraphs 3.14–3.23 the information the court needs to have about the offender and the offence; paragraphs 3.24–3.32 deferment, pronouncing sentence, amending sentence and appeal by the prosecution.

1.3 *Chapters 4 to 8* discuss in turn the various non-custodial sentences available to the courts. The emphasis varies according to questions of particular significance for each sentence, but in each case the text describes the circumstances in which the sentence can be imposed; the limits on its amount of length; the obligations which the sentence places on the offender and the sanctions available for failure satisfactorily to comply with them. *Chapters 9 and 10*, which deal with the custodial sentences which are the severest punishment available to the courts, concentrate more on the circumstances in which the sanction is justified, the criteria relevant to determining sentence length and the various different kinds of custodial order. *Chapter 9* considers suspension; partial suspension; extended sentences and life sentences, while *Chapter 10* covers young offender institutions, custody for life and detention of juveniles under the Children and Young Persons Act 1933.

1.4 *Chapters 11 and 12* focus on two groups of offenders for whom considerations other than deterrence and retribution are particularly relevant in sentencing: juveniles and mentally disordered offenders respectively. In each case the special considerations are reflected in special sentencing powers and procedural arrangements, and these are set out.

1.5 *Chapters 13 to 15* deal with various ancillary powers of wide application (rather than tied to particular offences): disqualification from driving (*Chapter 13*); recommendations for deportation (*Chapter 14*); restitution, forfeiture; and exclusion orders (*Chapter 15*).

1.6 The text has been written to be as self-contained as possible, with as little reference as possible to figures, statutes and other detailed sources. The Appendices seek to provide the most relevant background material: *Appendix 1* lists the sentences available to courts dealing with offenders in particular age groups; *Appendix 2* presents in tabular form a summary of the sentences passed by the courts in England and Wales in 1988, *Appendix 3* records the average costs of the sentences which involve the continuing provision of resources to carry them out. The *Bibliography* is organised according the chapter headings of the text and lists the main statutory and other sources of further information about the topics they consider.

CHAPTER 2

The Criminal Court System

The Court Heirarchy

2.1 Most criminal cases are tried, and the defendants, if convicted, sentenced, in magistrates' courts, which in 1988 prosecuted 1.9 million offenders and passed sentence on 1.5 million. Magistrates' powers to try cases and of punishment are limited, and more serious cases are dealt with by the Crown Court – ie by a judge (sitting in some instances with magistrates) and, if guilt is contested, a jury. The Crown Court also hears appeals by defendants against either conviction or sentence by magistrates' courts. In doing so it rehears the case and may impose any penalty which was available to the magistrates. In 1988 110,600 offenders appeared before the Crown Court and sentence was passed on 98,400. It is with the sentencing powers of these Courts that this book is concerned.

2.2 There are, however, three higher, appellate courts (all sitting in London) which oversee their work. The Divisional Court of the Queen's Bench Division of the High Court hears appeals on points of law and procedure, by either prosecution or defence, in cases originally dealt with by magistrates. The Court of Appeal, Criminal Division hears appeals from the Crown Court by the defendant against either conviction or sentence. In doing so the Court of Appeal may, from time to time, issue explicit guidance to the lower courts on the appropriate use of sentencing powers, and on many occasions the text of this booklet will refer to such advice. Under the provisions of the Criminal Justice Act 1988 cases can also be referred to the Court of Appeal by the Attorney General if it appears to him that the sentencing of a person for an offence triable only on indictment has been unduly lenient. The House of Lords is the final appeal court for all cases, from a decision either of the High Court or of the Court of Appeal. But before a case may proceed to the House of Lords, the court hearing the previous appeal must certify that it involves a point of law of general public importance, and either that court or the House of Lords must grant leave for the appeal to be heard.

The categories of offence

2.3 Trial by magistrates is known as summary trial; trial by the Crown

3

Court as trial on indictment. Criminal offences are grouped into three basic categories. Most offences have maximum penalties within the normal limits of magistrates' powers – a fine of up to £2000; custody for up to 6 months – and may be tried only summarily. These are known as summary offences. The offences which may be tried by the Crown Court – indictable offences – may vary greatly in seriousness. Examples of these are theft; burglary; malicious wounding; and indecent assault. These offences may be tried either summarily or on indictment, according to the circumstances of the case, and they are therefore known as offences triable either way. (Criminal damage, another common charge, is a special case. It is triable only summarily if the value of property involved does not exceed £2000; otherwise it is triable either way.) A few crimes – the most serious – are triable only on indictment. These offences include murder, manslaughter, rape and robbery.

Committal by Magistrates to Crown Court
2.4   There are four situations in which a magistrates' court may commit a case to be dealt with by the Crown Court.

a   where the offence is triable only on indictment, and the magistrates' hearing only a preliminary one;

b   where the offence is triable either way, and the defendant is committed for trial on indictment;

c   where the offence is triable either way and the defendant is tried summarily, but committed to the Crown Court for sentence;

d   certain other circumstances laid down in the Criminal Justice Act 1988

These are considered in turn in the following paragraphs.

2.5   Where the offence may only be tried on indictment, the magistrates' court decides preliminary matters such as whether the accused person is to be held in custody until trial or release on bail, and whether to grant legal aid. Where an accused person is legally represented a magistrates' court may, with his agreement,commit him to the Crown Court for trial without any consideration of the evidence. In all other cases the magistrates' court must examine the strength of the evidence and decide whether it warrants committal for trial. If not, the defendant has to be discharged.

2.6   If the offence is one triable either way, magistrates have to follow a set procedure in considering whether to try the case themselves or to commit it to the Crown Court for trial. Firstly the prosecution and defence have to be invited to indicate whether in their view the case is one which may suitably be dealt with summarily. It is important that the magistrates fully inform themselves at this stage of the gravity of the alleged crime, since their opportunity later on to commit the case to the Crown Court, where more severe penalties are available, is very limited.If after hearing both sides the magistrates feel that the case is too serious for them to deal with within their powers of punishment, they should proceed to commit the case to the Crown Court for trial.

2.7 If they regard the case as suitable for summary trial, the magistrates must explain to the defendant that he can either consent to be tried by them or may exercise the right to trial by jury. Depending on what he elects, the magistrates' court then proceeds to try him or commit him for trial to the Crown Court.

2.8 If the defendant consents to summary trial and pleads guilty to the offence charged, the case may not subsequently be committed for trial to the Crown Court. Where the defendant consents to summary trial but contests the charge, the magistrates may decide, at any time during the presentation of the prosecution case, that the charge should after all be tried on indictment, and may commit the case for trial to the Crown Court.

2.9 In making the decision to try the case summarily, the magistrates have no knowledge of the defendant's circumstances and any previous convictions. This information will be presented if the defendant is convicted, and the court may feel that in the light of it a more severe sentence than it has power to impose is appropriate. In such a case the defendant – who must be warned about this possibility when being asked whether he consents to summary trial – may be committed for sentence to the Crown Court, which may pass any sentence which it could have done had the trial and conviction been on indictment.

2.10 If an offender is charged with an indictable offence and also with certain specified summary offences, then under section 40 of the Criminal Justice Act 1988 the summary offences may be included as additional counts on the indictment. This applies only when the summary offence is part of a series of offences of a similar character to the indictable offence, or is founded on the same facts or evidence as the indictable offence. The summary offence is then tried as if it were an indictable offence, but the offender may only be dealt with for it as if he were being tried in the magistrates' court. The summary offences to which this applies are those of taking a motor vehicle or other conveyance without authority; driving whilst disqualified; summary criminal damage and associated offences; and common assault.

2.11   Frequently an accused person will be charged with several offences, some of them triable either way and some summarily. A magistrates' court, when committing a person to the Crown Court for trial for an offence which is triable either way, may also commit him for trial for any summary offence which appears to arise out of circumstances connected with the either way offence, and which is punishable with imprisonment or disqualification (obligatory or discretionary) from driving. If the defendant is convicted on the indictment, and pleads guilty to the summary offence, the Crown Court may deal with him for the summary offence in the same manner as a magistrates' court could have dealt with him.

2.12   If the magistrates wish to commit an offender found guilty of an either way offence to the Crown Court for sentencing, they are not obliged to proceed to pass sentence on him for any associated summary offences, of which he has also been found guilty, but may commit him to the Crown Court for sentencing him for all the offences. In passing sentence the Crown Court may not exceed the maximum penalties available to the magistrates.

2.13   Special arrangements apply to juveniles – see paragraph 11.5.

CHAPTER 3

Sentences and Sentencing

3.1   Before proceeding to the rest of the book, which outlines the various powers available to the courts, it is necessary to consider the basic general principles and procedures which should be applied in the task of choosing the appropriate sentence for a particular case. In doing so, this chapter considers the general theoretical aims of sentencing; the rationale of the various specific options which are available; the court's gathering of information to assist it in the sentencing decision, and various ancillary aspects of the decision itself.

The aims of sentencing
3.2   The criminal courts play a key role in the criminal justice system. The objectives of that system are to prevent, detect and punish crimes, and other agencies – such as the police, the prison service and the probation service – are involved in seeking to achieve them. The sanctions available to the courts are designed at least partly as punishments, but it is natural to ask to what extent they also serve to prevent crime. There are three ways in which they might be expected to do so: by deterring potential offenders generally, through fear of punishment; by influencing offenders who have been appropriately sentenced not to offend again; and by putting out of circulation, through custody, those who are a particular nuisance or a particular danger. The research evidence, however, suggests that within the realistic range of choice, imposing particular sentences, or particularly severe sentences, has a very limited effect on crime levels.

3.3   The simplest way of evaluating the individual deterrent effect of sentencing is to compare the proportions of offenders undergoing different types of sentence who, when free to do so, continue to commit offences. The almost invariable conclusion of the large amount of research which has been undertaken (in various Western countries) is that it is hard to show any effect that one type of sentence is more likely than any other to reduce the likelihood of reoffending, which is high for all. Similarly, longer periods of custody or particular institutional regimes do not seem to have a significant effect. Studies comparing the reconviction rates of offenders given community service orders with those given custodial sentences have also shown little difference.

3.4   The general deterrent effect is in principle very difficult to measure, and this may in part account for the fact that there is also no clear evidence associating sentence severity and crime rates. But it is also true that such an effect can only occur for criminal acts which are premeditated by people making rational calculations of the likelihood of being caught, the likely sentence and the likely benefits from the crime. The inference most commonly drawn from research studies is that the probability of arrest and conviction is likely to deter potential offenders, whereas the perceived severity of the ensuing penalties has little effect.

3.5   The incapacitation effect of custody of course operates whatever the deterrent effect – the offender is taken away from society. But it is modest. A Home Office study has estimated that if all sentences of imprisonment were reduced by 6 months (4 months actually served, when remission of sentence is taken into account), the annual increase in convictions would be only 1.6 per cent. These findings omit offences which are not 'cleared up', and should therefore be viewed with caution. They do, however, suggest that no realistic increase in prison terms would make a substantial impact on crime rates simply by virtue of locking up the particular offenders caught, convicted and sentenced.

3.6   It is, of course, very difficult in conducting studies of this kind to adjust for all the potentially relevant variables, and it would be wrong to conclude from these results that sentences are never an effective deterrent in individual cases or that deterrence is not relevant to sentencing – still less that the general deterrent effect on the population of the existing structure of penalties is non-existent. What they might be taken to suggest is rather that a sentence should not normally be justified on merely deterrent or therapeutic grounds – either that the offender will be 'cured' or that others need to be discouraged from similar crimes. Properly reflecting the relative gravity of the offence, and fairness between different offenders, are more important aims in the individual case.

The choice of a type of penalty
3.7   It is with regard to custody, the most severe penalty open to the Courts, that these factors are particularly relevant. It would be wrong to impose a custodial sentence when such a severe penalty was not warranted by the gravity of the offence merely in the hope of achieving a deterrent or reformative effect which experience suggests is unlikely to occur. As Appendix 3 shows, a custodial sentence is by far the most expensive type of sentence. A custodial sentence is also the most likely to have unwanted side-effects. It is likely to affect an offender's personal or financial prospects. There is the possibility that serious hardship will be inflicted on the offender's family, particularly those responsible for the care of young

children. The Court of Appeal (in the 1976 case of R v Parkinson) stated that, in certain circumstances, the family responsibilities of a female offender may be treated as a mitigating factor. The sentence may take account of the effect on the offender's family when sentencing a woman who is the mother of young children. On release from custody, it can be very difficult for the offender to be re-integrated in the community. Furthermore, for the young or inexperienced offender, mixing with more sophisticated inmates may deepen his anti-social attitudes and increase his criminal skills. All these considerations are summed up in the general principle, laid down by the Court of Appeal, that custody should only be used when it is really necessary and, if imposed, the sentence should be as short as is consistent with the need for punishment. (R v Upton, 1980).

3.8   There are, of course, certain offences, such as rape and trafficking in heroin or cocaine, which are so serious in themselves that custody is virtually inevitable. The Court of Appeal has in fact given specific guidance for these particular offences, listing the main aggravating and mitigating factors which determine the severity of the offence and thus the likely range of sentence length. Most imprisonable offences , however, will only merit the use of custody for the more serious instances. For some of them, the Court of Appeal has given guidance as to those aggravating features likely to justify the use of a custodial sentence. For causing death by reckless driving, for example, the aggravating factors were listed by the Court as including: the consumption of alcohol or drugs; racing or competitive driving against another vehicle on the public highway; grossly excessive speed, or showing off; disregarding warnings from passengers, or otherwise being persistent and deliberate in the reckless driving; committing other road traffic offences at the same time; previous convictions for bad driving or for consuming excessive alcohol before driving; causing the deaths of several people in the same incident; behaving badly after the incident (eg failing to stop, or trying to 'throw off' the victim from the bonnet of the car); causing death while driving recklessly in trying to avoid detection or apprehension.

3.9   The aim of guidance of this kind, on this as on other aspects of sentencing, is not to secure uniformity of sentence, but rather to promote uniformity of approach. Much will always depend on the particular circumstances of the individual offender and the individual offence, which will together determine the gravity of the misconduct. But the court should always satisfy itself before imposing custody that there is a positive justification for doing so. Where the crime is one which appears to demand anything up to 2 years' imprisonment, but the personal circumstances of an (adult) offender suggest that it would be unnecessarily harsh to exact that penalty in the particular case, the court may suspend the sentence, wholly or in part. This and other details of courts' powers to imprison offenders are discussed in Chapter 9 (and Chapter 10 so far as young offenders, are concerned). But it is worth noting here that even for indictable offences, immediate custody was only found to be necessary in 17% of cases in 1988. For those indictable offences which (being triable either way) were dealt with by magistrates' courts, the proportion was only 7%.

3.10 It is also important to remember, especially given the findings discussed in paragraphs 3.2–3.6 above, that the use of non-custodial penalties should mark the gravity of the offence as well as the 'fit' of the sentence with the particular offender. There will be cases in which the offence is sufficiently trivial, or, in the circumstances, excusable, for it to be unnecessary to impose punishment beyond the conviction itself. The appropriate order is then an absolute or conditional discharge (see Chapter 4). If the offence is more serious, but not such as to warrant custody, a fine, a purely punitive order, will often be the most suitable penalty. Provided the offender has means, this is a simple and practical response to the offence. As Chapter 5 discusses in more detail, the fine should be set at a level reflecting the gravity of the offence, reduced if necessary where the offender has little money available. Where a financial penalty cannot realistically be imposed because of the offender's circumstances, another non-custodial penalty should be chosen instead (see paragraph 5.17).

3.11 The community service order (Chapter 7) and the attendance centre order (Chapter 8) may only be imposed for offences which are imprisonable. Community service is only available for offenders aged 16 or over; attendance centres for offenders aged under 21. Each of these penalties is punitive and the offender's conduct should have been serious enough to warrant depriving him of freedom of action at specified times. The activity undertaken in fulfilling these orders is designed to be as constructive as possible, but also to make real demands on the offender. Community service has the added element of requiring something to be given back to the community. This more positive and direct punishment should normally be reserved for offences where a fine will not meet the gravity of the case, and so far as community service is concerned the Court of Appeal has specifically said that in a case where some months' imprisonment seems justified the court should ask itself whether a community service order might not as effectively serve the same punitive purpose.

3.12 Some sanctions stand largely outside this 'tariff' reflecting the gravity of the offence, and are designed for cases in which factors other than punishment are particularly important. The probation order (Chapter 6) will be a suitable alternative where the offender's personal difficulties have loomed large in the case and it seems that professional supervision would help to overcome them. It remains, however, an order of the court, and the conditions attached to it must be complied with for the period specified; sanctions are available if they are breached. It may thus be an appropriate sanction in some cases where the offence is a serious one and custody would have been justified. Mentally disordered offenders (Chapter 12) may require medical treatment rather than punishment. And in any case where the offence has caused clear and specific harm to victims the court must consider making a compensation order (see Chapter 5) in their favour.

3.13   Special considerations and some special sentences, apply to juvenile offenders. See Chapter 11.

Information for sentencing

A   The facts of the offence
3.14   Information about the facts of the offence will normally be provided by the prosecution. If the accused person has pleaded not guilty and has been convicted after a trial the court will have heard the evidence about the offence in the course of the trial and will not normally need any further information about it. But in most cases the offender will have pleaded guilty. The prosecution will then open the case by giving the court an outline of the facts of the offence, in the form of a summary of the evidence. Usually there will be no objections to the prosecution's account, but the accused person, whilst admitting the offence, may dispute the detailed version of the facts put before the court – for example, the amount of property involved in a theft; whether a weapon was used in an assault. Where there are such differences on matters relevant to sentence, the court must resolve them before imposing sentence. Unless a contested point is proved by the prosecution to the court's satisfaction, it cannot be taken into account in passing sentence. If witnesses on the matter are available, the court may proceed to invite the prosecution and defence to call and question them, as in a contested trial. If they are not, and the point is of sufficient significance, the case may need to be adjourned.

3.15   A defendant pleading guilty to an offence may wish to admit other similar ones. It may well not be convenient to prefer formal charges for every offence, and the courts have accordingly developed the practice of taking offences into consideration, which allows the defendant to be dealt with for all of a series of similar offences without being formally convicted of them. The prosecution prepare a list of the other offences, and should give the defendant a copy of the list some days before the court hearing. If the defendant is willing to admit the further offences, he signs the list, which is then put before the court. The court should, before passing sentence, ask the defendant to confirm admission of the offences on the list. If there is any doubt about which offences are admitted, the defendant should be asked to identify them, individually if necessary. Once the admitted offences to be taken into consideration have been established, the court may proceed to sentence for the offences formally charged, and in doing so may pass a more severe sentence than it would have done on the facts of those offences alone. (The maximum sentence, however, remains that for the offence or offences formally charged.) A typical example is where an employee is charged with a small theft from his employer and admits a series of similar offences on earlier occasions. The court is entitled in sentencing to take account of the total amount stolen in the whole course of the admitted offending. Although no separate sentence may be passed for offences taken into consideration, the court may order an offender to pay compensation for any loss, damage or personal injury resulting from them. There is no statutory basis for this procedure, but the established practice is that the offender will not be prosecuted again for any offences taken into consideration, and will be treated afterwards for all practical purposes as if he had been convicted of the offences. The prosecution has agreed to the use of the 'taking into consideration' procedure, and the offender's punishment has taken the crimes concerned into account.

B *The circumstances of the offender*
3.16 Information about the offender is provided from a number of sources. The prosecution will provide a statement known as 'the antecedents'. This amounts to a brief account of the defendant's history; domestic circumstances and previous convictions and sentences, if any. This will normally be derived from interviews with the defendant, supplemented by police records and such separate police verification of particulars as has been possible. Again, the defence may seek to dispute, supplement or further explain this account, and the court must carefully assess the available information. The scope for enquiry may be limited by the fact that, at any rate in a magistrates' court, the police officer presenting evidence is unlikely to have personal knowledge of the offender concerned.

3.17 Where the defendant is convicted of a serious offence, however, a social inquiry report, giving fuller information about the background and circumstances of the offender, will usually be prepared for the court by a probation officer or, sometimes, in cases involving juveniles a local authority social worker. Though there is no standard form for such reports, they normally contain information about the character, personality and social and domestic background of the defendant; his educational record and information from his most recent employer (if any) about his employment prospects and approach to work. This information will be gathered by the probation officer in interviews with the defendant and others with relevant information. The report may include some comments on possible sentences which the court may consider. It is accepted as proper practice for the probation officer to include in the report an opinion on the likely response of the offender to probation, and, if the court wishes, any other form of treatment, if the probation officer's knowledge or experience makes this possible. It is not usually considered to be the responsibility of the probation officer to offer comments on the gravity of the offence in mitigation of the offender's conduct, nor to advise on the question whether the treatment of the offender is the aspect of sentencing to which the court should give priority.

3.18   A copy of any social inquiry report prepared in a case must be given to the offender or the offender's legal representative. The prosecution do not normally receive a copy. Social inquiry reports are not read aloud in court, but the defence may question the officers who present them about the contents.

3.19   Some kinds of sentence may not normally be passed unless the court has considered a social inquiry report on the offender. For community service orders, this is a statutory requirement. Certain custodial sentences may not be imposed unless the court has considered a report in order to determine whether there is any other means of dealing with the offender. This requirement, which is designed to reinforce the need for great care in the use of custody, does not apply if the court 'considers it unnecessary' to consider a report; a magistrates' court which imposes any of these sentences without obtaining a social inquiry report must, however, state in open court its reasons for considering it unnecessary to do so. The categories of custodial sentences concerned are:

(a) a sentence of imprisonment (even if wholly or partly suspended) on a person who has not previously served a sentence of immediate imprisonment (as an adult).

(b) any custodial sentence on an offender aged under 21.

Although there is no statutory requirement to do so, it will also normally be appropriate to obtain a social inquiry report before making a probation order on an offender – professional advice from what would be the supervising service on the offender's suitability for the order is obviously highly desirable.

Another circumstance in which it will normally be appropriate to obtain a report, though there is again no statutory requirement to do so, is where a magistrates' court is considering committal to the Crown Court for sentence.

3.20   These categories are not exhaustive. There may well be other cases in which it is likely to be of assistance to the court that any significant factors about the offender's background are brought to the court's notice. The Home Office has, for example, suggested that magistrates should normally obtain a report before passing any sentence of imprisonment on a woman. This will enable the court to consider whether her family responsibilities should be treated as a mitigating factor (see paragraph 3.7).

3.21   A further source of information about the offender will be material presented directly by the defence in mitigation. An offender charged with a serious offence will almost certainly be legally represented for this purpose, either by a barrister (counsel) or by a solicitor. The defence lawyer may present information directly, and will in any event make a speech in mitigation on behalf of the offender. This speech will try to give the court the defendant's explanation of the offence and any matters in the defendant's favour. It may be supported by the testimony of witnesses or by evidence in some other form; certainly assertions concerning the conduct or character of the offender or other parties are unlikely to weigh heavily with the court unless substantiated.

3.22   Some disposals available to the court may not be imposed on an offender who is not legally represented. These are:

(a) a sentence of imprisonment (even if wholly or partly suspended) on a person who has not previously served a sentence of immediate imprisonment (as an adult);

(b) any custodial sentence on an offender aged under 21;

(c) a care order, or a charge and control condition attached to a care order, made on a juvenile (see Chapter 11).

Such sentences may only be passed in these categories of case if the offender has been legally represented in the proceedings between conviction and sentence. (This rule does not, however, apply when the defendant has effectively decided against being represented: the two categories of such cases being where he has refused to apply for legal aid after being informed of the right to do so and where his application for legal aid has been refused because his financial circumstances were such that assistance was not necessary.)

Adjournment for reports

3.23   The court may decide on hearing the information put before it that it needs further information before deciding what sentence to impose. It may in such circumstances adjourn the case until that information can be obtained. Sometimes the need may not be for an elaborate enquiry – such as would, for example, be required for a full-scale social inquiry or medical report – but for basic information which can be readily obtained or checked. In such a case the court may adjourn the case until later in the same sitting while a 'stand down' report is obtained by the probation service representative in court. Otherwise the adjournment may be until such later date as seems reasonable. A magistrates' court is limited to a period of four weeks at a time, or three weeks if the offender is remanded in custody, although the case may if necessary be remanded on more than one occasion. When the defendant reappears before the court, a different judge or magistrates may be sitting; if so, they may pass sentence. This makes it the more important that the court which adjourns the case is careful not to give the offender the impression that it has provisionally decided to impose a particular kind of sentence – eg community service or probation – if the information in the report is favourable. Otherwise, the court which is finally required to deal with the case may feel bound to honour that implied recommendation even if it would itself have preferred a different sentence.

Deferment of sentence

3.24   An adjournment for reports is to seek more information. Quite different is the courts' power to defer passing sentence for a specified period of up to six months. This is designed to meet the case where because of what the court has discovered about the offender it feels it right to postpone the sentencing decision in order to 'have regard . . . . to his conduct after conviction, (including where appropriate the making by him of any reparation for his offence) or to any change in his circumstances'. The use of this power requires the defendant's consent. It may be summarised as an agreement between the court and the defendant that if the defendant does what is expected of him during the deferment, he will not receive the severe sentence – normally one of custody – which the offence might otherwise warrant.

3.25   The Court of Appeal has given detailed guidance on the use of this power, which may be summarised as follows:

(a)   deferment is not to be used as a means of avoiding making a difficult sentencing decision. There must be specific reasons to believe that it would be in the interests of justice to postpone judgement in order to take account of some intended conduct by

15

the defendant or some change in his circumstances. That reason would normally have emerged from the defendant's conduct between the offence and the hearing of the case;

(b) deferment should not be used simply in order to secure performance by the defendant of a specific task which could be clearly defined as a condition of a probation order (eg continuing a course of medical treatment; residence at a specific hostel)

(c) deferment may, however, be appropriate where it would not be easy, or valid, to make the conduct desirable a specific requirement of an order. Making a real effort to find work, or maintaining a changed attitude or new position would be examples of expectations too general to be incorporated as conditions of a probation order; realizing an expressed intention to make reparation to the victim, for example, is not necessarily within an offender's power to deliver;

(d) nevertheless, it is essential for a court which defers sentence to make it clear to the defendant what particular purposes the court has in mind and what conduct is expected during the period of deferment. The court should make a careful note of its reasons, and make it clear to the offender what object it has in mind in deferring sentence. It is also important for all concerned to be clear that deferment of sentence is a postponement of the sentencing decision and not in itself a sentence. This serves to avoid the risk of misunderstanding, and the resultant sense of injustice, when the defendant eventually returns for sentence.

3.26 At the end of the period of deferment, the defendant appears again before the court and a sentence is imposed for the original offence. The court has no power to order the defendant to appear before the end of the period of deferment, but if he is convicted of another offence during that period the court dealing with the later offence may also pass sentence for the one which was the subject of the deferment. (The court may only defer sentence once on an offender appearing before it.) When the defendant appears to be dealt with following the deferment, the sentencing court should first discover the reason for the deferment and the nature of any requirements imposed on the defendant and then determine whether the defendant has substantially kept his side of the 'bargain' by doing what was expected. If he has, the defendant may legitimately expect not to be sent into custody. If not, the court should state precisely in what respect he has failed, so that he is in no doubt that it has fully considered the purposes of the original, deferring court in making its decision. (It is not, of course, in any way bound then to pass a custodial sentence – it may impose any penalty open to the deferring court.)

Pronouncing sentence

3.27 Sentence is pronounced in open court (though the court may previously have retired to consider its decision), and it is recorded by the clerk –in writing. The court is not always required to give reasons for its sentence, but it may often, especially in more serious cases, be appropriate to do so. There are three particular classes of case where giving an explanation is especially desirable, or necessary: where the sentence is one which makes specific requirements of the offender; where the sentence is one which requires statutory justification; where the sentence is one which is liable to be misunderstood by the public.

3.28 The first class includes conditional discharges; probation orders; community service orders; wholly or partly suspended prison sentences and charge and control conditions in care orders imposed on juveniles. In each case the defendant must be clear what is being required, and what consequences may follow failure to comply with the court's order. In each case the court is obliged by law to explain the sentence's effect in ordinary language.

3.29 The second class includes: (a) the use of custody for certain kinds of offender and (b) a departure from a statutory presumption that a certain course will be followed. Magistrates' courts must state reasons why no other order is appropriate before imposing a custodial sentence on any person under twenty-one years' old or passing a prison sentence (whether or not suspended) on any adult who has not served a previous term in prison. The Crown Court must give reasons for imposing a sentence of detention in a young offender institution. Decisions which require explanation as departing from the normal course are: not activating in full a suspended sentence, or the suspended portion of a partly suspended sentence, when the defendant has reoffended during the period of suspension, and not disqualifying from driving a defendant convicted of an offence for which disqualification is normally obligatory.

3.30 The third class includes particular cases which without explanation might seem excessively lenient – such as a comparatively modest fine which has been substantially reduced because of the offender's means but still represents, in effect, a heavy penalty for him.

Amending the sentence

3.31 Both magistrates' courts and the Crown Court may alter the sentence they have imposed on an offender, provided they do so within twenty-eight days of originally imposing it. (For the Crown Court, the time limit is extended for defendants tried jointly with others to twenty-eight days from the joint trial or fifty-six days from the date on which the sentence in question was passed, whichever is the shorter.) Commonly, though not necessarily exclusively, this power is required to correct an inadvertent mistake, where the court has exceeded its power or in some other way acted on a misunderstanding. A magistrates' court which alters its sentence must include either the same magistrates as the original one or, if there were three, at least two of them. A Crown Court sentence must be altered by the judge who imposed it, though this may be done in the absence of one or more of any magistrates who may also have been sitting on the original bench.

Appeal by the prosecution
3.32   A case heard in the Crown Court may be referred to the Court of Appeal by the Attorney General if it appears to him that the sentence passed for an offence triable only on indictment has been unduly lenient. The Court of Appeal may quash the original sentence and, in place of it, pass such a sentence as they think appropriate.

CHAPTER 4

Discharges and Binding Over

Absolute and conditional discharges

4.1 An order discharging a person absolutely or conditionally is appropriate where the court takes the view, having regard to the circumstances including the nature of the offence and the character of the offender, that it is inexpedient to inflict punishment and that a probation order is not appropriate.

4.2 An absolute discharge (which is not to be confused with a finding of not guilty) is used where the court, having found the offender guilty of the offence charged, considers that no further action is required on its part beyond the finding of guilt. This may reflect the triviality of the offence, the circumstances in which it came to be prosecuted, or factors relating to the offender.

4.3 An order for conditional discharge similarly imposes no obligation on the offender, except that he remains liable to punishment for the offence if, within whatever period of not more than three years the court may specify, he is convicted of a further offence. Before making an order for conditional discharge, the court is required to explain to the offender in ordinary language that if he commits another offence during the period of conditional discharge he will be liable to be sentenced for the original offence. When a person is sentenced for the original offence, the order for conditional discharge ceases to have effect.

4.4 An order for a conditional discharge differs from a bind-over (see paragraphs 4.6 to 4.8) in that the condition attached relates to the commission of a further offence. It differs from a probation order (see Chapter 6) in three respects: it may be applied to a person under the age of 17; it involves no continuing supervision of the offender; and only one condition – that the offender does not commit another offence – can be imposed. It differs from a suspended sentence (see paragraphs 9.10 to 9.16 below) in that if the offender commits a further offence during the period of discharge there is no statutory obligation on the court to deal with him for his original offence, and if it does so the sentence is not pre-determined (as with a suspended sentence) but is considered afresh by the court. The conditional discharge is quite widely used, especially in relation to juveniles, in circumstances where the court judges it unnecessary to impose any sanction on the convicted person provided he commits no further offence during the period specified. In 1988, 4 per cent of adults and 28 per cent of juveniles found guilty in magistrates' courts were dealt with in this way.

4.5 The court may accompany an order for absolute or conditional discharge with an order to pay compensation or costs or to restore stolen property.

Binding over
4.6 Instead of imposing punishment the Crown Court may, except in a case of murder, require an offender to enter into a recognisance with or without sureties to come up for judgement when called upon. When a person enters into a recognisance, he is said to be 'bound over'. By this he recognises that a failure to comply with conditions stated by the court will cause him to forfeit a sum of money stipulated by the court in the order of binding over. The recognisance may also require the offender to keep the peace and/or be of good behaviour; if he does not comply with this requirement, the money involved may be forfeited and he may be brought before the court and dealt with for the original offence. An offender under recognisance differs from a conditionally discharged offender in that he may be brought back to court at any time and dealt with without having been convicted of a further offence; the court has to be satisfied, on complaint, only that he has failed to keep the peace or be of good behaviour.

4.7 All courts have power, in certain circumstances, to require that an offender shall enter into a recognisance, with or without sureties, to keep the peace and be of good behaviour. This power is of ancient origin and is referred to in the Justices of the Peace Act 1361. A person aged 17 or over ordered by a court to enter into a recognisance who refuses to comply with the order may be committed to custody for a period not exceeding 6 months or until he or she complies with the order. A person who has entered into a recognisance but subsequently breaches its condition may be ordered to forfeit the sum of money required to be paid by the recognisance.

4.8 If a juvenile is found guilty of an offence, an order requiring a parent or guardian to enter into a recognisance to take proper care of and exercise proper control over him may be made, if the parent or guardian consents.

A recognisance on a parent or guardian may not exceed £1000 and may be made for up to three years or until the juvenile attains the age of 18, whichever is the shorter period.

CHAPTER 5

Financial Penalties

Compensation orders

5.1   Where an offence has caused loss, damage or personal injury to someone, the court is required to consider whether the offender should pay compensation for that person's benefit. A compensation order may be the only sentence for the offence, or it may be made in addition to any other sentence (including a probation order or discharge) which the court thinks appropriate, except a criminal bankruptcy order. (The court's power to award compensation, does, however, depend upon convicting the offender.) The order may be enforced following conviction, but the person in whose favour the order is made is not entitled to receive any payments until an appeal against the order is no longer possible. Where a court considers both a compensation order and a fine appropriate, but the offender's means are not adequate to pay both in full, the court is required to give preference to the ordering of compensation. Where the court decides not to make any order for compensation it must give reasons. Where a compensation order is made against a juvenile, the court *must* order his parent or guardian to pay, unless it would be unreasonable to do so in the circumstances or the parent or guardian cannot be found.

5.2   Where the victim of the offence has been killed, compensation may be awarded for funeral expenses or bereavement unless death was due to the presence of a motor vehicle on the road in which case claims can be met under insurance arrangements. Compensation for funeral expenses may be ordered for the benefit of whoever incurred them. Compensation for bereavement can be made to the relatives and dependants of the deceased up to the amount specified in Section 1A(3) of the Fatal Accidents Act 1976 (£3,500). Where the loss, damage or injury arises out of the presence of a vehicle on road, a compensation order may only be made for damage resulting from an offence under the Theft Act 1968 or for loss, damage or personal injury for which the offender is uninsured and where compensation is not payable under the Motor Insurers' Bureau Agreement. In such cases compensation may include any loss or reduction in preferential rates of insurance (no claims bonus.)

22

5.3 The particular value of the compensation order is in dealing with a relatively simple case, in which the amount of damage can be clearly determined. The making of a compensation order enables the victim to obtain speedy redress without having to institute civil proceedings, and allows the court to bring home directly to the offender the harm done to the victim. The general power to award compensation does not affect the victim's rights in civil law although the civil courts will take into account any compensation already paid by the offender to avoid double compensation.

5.4 The Crown Court may award any amount of compensation, up to the amount of the loss, damage or injury; the magistrates' court may award up to £2,000 for any one offence. The court can order the defendant to pay compensation for the loss, damage or injury caused by offences which it has been asked to take into consideration, as well as for those of which it has actually convicted the defendant. In such a case, however, the total amount which a magistrates' court may award is limited to the maximum it could order for the offences of which the offender has been formally convicted. If, for example, the offender is convicted of six offences and asks for another four to be taken into consideration, the total amount which it may order for the ten offences is £12,000 – six times £2,000.

5.5 Compensation ordered by a court is quite different from compensation payable by the Criminal Injuries Compensation Board. The Board administers a publicly-funded scheme under which victims of violent crime can be compensated whether or not the assailant is caught or convicted. The terms of the scheme define when compensation is payable but the assessment of the amount of damages is made on the same basis as the civil courts. There is a lower limit of £550 which means that a victim who suffers only minor injury will not be eligible for compensation from the Board; however that should not deter the court from making a compensation order in appropriate cases. When the Board awards compensation in a case where a court has made a compensation order the Board will pay any court compensation still owing and recover through the victim or the court further payments made by the offender.

5.6 Before making a compensation order, the court must first satisfy itself that actual loss, damage or injury has resulted from the offence which the offender has committed. Loss may include such things as the value of goods which have been stolen; the cost of repairing or replacing things which have been damaged; loss of wages through time off work following an assault. It may also include matters for which it is more difficult to fix a value, such as pain and suffering, shock or disablement. Guidance on the assessment of compensation is given in Home Office circular 85/88.

5.7 The court's next task is to settle the amount of the loss, damage or injury for which the offender may be required to pay compensation. In doing this, the court should consider whatever evidence it feels may assist its assessment, subject to the rights of prosecution and defence to make representations and to question witnesses. (The victim does not have any distinctive rights to the case, and is not a party to the proceedings, though of course the victim may be called upon to give evidence.) Parliament has relaxed the strict rule applied by the courts until recently, that the amount of the loss, damage or injury should always be fully proved unless it is agreed between the prosecution and defendant, but the Court of Appeal has stated that the relaxation of this requirement does not mean that courts can simply decide a figure by guesswork. There must be some basis for the award in evidence of the extent of the loss, damage or injury, though the amount need not be proved quite as strictly as other matters in criminal cases are required to be.

5.8 If the court is satisfied that damage, loss or injury of a certain value has been caused, it should also, before making a compensation order, consider the financial circumstances of the offender. Parliament has provided that in determining whether to make a compensation order, and in fixing the amount of the order, the court 'shall have regard to his means so far as they appear or are known to the court'. The Court of Appeal has interpreted this to mean that a compensation order should be such as to enable the offender to complete payment within a reasonable time. It is wrong in principle to make a compensation order for an amount that the offender has no hope of paying, or for an amount which will involve payment by instalments over too long a period. But the courts have not ruled out payment over a period as long as three years where appropriate. Courts need not, however, be deterred from making a compensation order simply because the offender cannot make good the whole sum involved. An order for part of the sum will still be appropriate if otherwise justified. If there is more than one victim, but the offender's means are not sufficient to enable him to compensate them all, the usual procedure is to scale down the amount to be paid in each case. But when this approach would mean that some victims would receive very small sums, it may sometimes be better to select some victims and to make compensation orders in favour of them only.

5.9 In deciding how much compensation the offender can afford to pay, the court may consider any savings or capital which he has available, and his expected income. The assets which may be taken into account are not limited to the proceeds of the crime. Sometimes an offender who is anxious to pay compensation intends to raise the money by selling some property, such as a car or motorcycle; the Court of Appeal has indicated that before a compensation order is made in such circumstances it should have a proper valuation of the property from someone with knowledge of the relevant trade, and not simply accept the offender's own valuation, which may be over-optimistic. If the offender is likely to have difficulty in selling the property, the court should not make a compensation order on the assumption that it will be sold – particularly where the property concerned is the family house, in which other people may have legal rights.

5.10   There are obvious difficulties in making compensation orders when offenders are sent to prison or some other form of custody. It is not necessarily wrong to make a compensation order in combination with a custodial sentence, but the court must be particularly careful to ensure that the offender has or will have the means to pay the amount ordered, usually from assets which are available at the time of the sentence. The Court of Appeal has indicated that it is wrong to make compensation orders which will simply be a burden to offenders on release from custody, as it may lead them to commit further offences to raise the money to pay off the orders. Nevertheless, where an offender who is paying compensation is subsequently imprisoned for another offence, it will not normally be appropriate (unless the beneficiary of the order agrees) to allow the outstanding amount of compensation owed to be 'extinguished' by imposing a concurrent prison term in default of payment. Compensation orders are enforced in the same way as fines – see paragraphs 5.21-5.32.

5.11   There is provision for a compensation order to be reviewed where a civil court has decided that the injury, loss or damage was less than that ordered by the criminal court; or where the property was recovered by the beneficiary of the order; or where the offender has suffered an unexpected and substantial reduction in means which is likely to continue for some time, or where the offender's means are insufficient to meet in full the compensation order and any confiscation order made under the Criminal Justice Act 1988 in the same proceedings.

Fines
5.12   A court may fine an offender for any offence (except murder or treason). There is no limit on the amount of the fine which the Crown Court may impose. The magistrates' court may fine an offender for any offence which it can deal with, but the amount which a magistrates' court may fine is limited, according to the offence or offences committed. With a very few exceptions, £2000 is the highest sum magistrates may fine for either way offences and it is also the value of the highest of the five points on the 'standard scale' of maximum fines on to which almost all maxima

for summary offences have been placed. The current values of the standard scale are: Level 1, £50; Level 2, £100; Level 3, £400; Level 4, £1000 and Level 5, £2000. The maximum fine that can be imposed on a young person (aged 14 to 16) is £400, whatever the offence, and a child (aged under 14) may not be fined more than £100. As with compensation orders, the court *must* order a fine imposed on a juvenile to be paid by his parent or guardian unless it would be unreasonable to do so in the circumstances or the parent or guardian cannot be found.

5.13 The fine is a purely punitive measure which enables the court to demonstrate society's disapproval of the offence in a case where punishment (short of custody) is the appropriate response. The court may impose a fine as an alternative to custody. However, it may not be combined for the same offence, with a discharge or a probation order – where the court decides that it is unnecessary to impose punishment – or with a community service order. For most imprisonable offences the court may impose a fine as well as custody, or a suspended prison sentence. This may be particularly appropriate where an offender has made a substantial profit from the offence. But before passing such a sentence, the offender's ability to pay the fine must be taken into account and, as with any custodial sentence, the court should satisfy itself that such a severe penalty is warranted (see paragraph 3.7). These considerations make it unusual for magistrates to impose both a fine and custody.

5.14 In deciding the amount of the fine, the first consideration must be the gravity of the offence. Is the case a more or less serious example of its kind, and what is the maximum fine? Clearly the penalty imposed must not exceed the sum arrived at by this means. The gravity of a particular offence will be affected by many different aggravating and mitigating factors relating to the offence and the offender. Amongst these will be any financial gain to the offender from the offence. The various relevant factors will clearly vary widely between cases, and fining should not be approached on a mechanistic basis. Nevertheless, particular magistrates' courts will often have developed recognised conventions from practice and experience over the years which can serve as a starting point in considering the range of fine levels for common offences. For some offences, the Magistrates' Association (a non-statutory body to which the majority of magistrates belong) has prepared a set of guidelines to which magistrates may refer in deciding how to approach the decision on the amount of a fine. As the Association's notes make clear, these guidelines are not intended to be followed rigidly. Their purpose is to provide starting points from which the court may calculate the penalty in the particular case. They are intended to assist courts to achieve as much consistency in the fines imposed in different parts of the country as is consistent with the exercise of judicial discretion in each individual case.

5.15   When an offender is charged on the same occasion with more than one offence, and is to be fined for each, it is particularly important (not least in road traffic cases) that the 'totality principle' be observed. That is to say, in considering the fine appropriate to the gravity of the offences, the court should consider the offending as a whole, rather than simply aggregating the figures which might be appropriate for each individual offence. The total fine imposed should not exceed that appropriate to the criminal conduct seen as a whole.

5.16   The court must then, before finally deciding on the appropriate sum, consider the financial circumstances of the offender. Parliament has provided specifically that a magistrates' court must, in fixing the amount of a fine, 'take into consideration among other things the means of the person on whom the fine is imposed so far as they appear or are known to the Court'. The Court of Appeal has many times confirmed that this principle also applies to the Crown Court. The Court has ruled that the gravity of the offence should always be the *first* consideration. It is therefore clearly not correct sentencing practice to increase the level of a fine beyond what is appropriate to the circumstances of the offence simply because an offender is very affluent. Moreover a fine should not be so heavy that it sends an offender to prison "by the back door" for default. It may, therefore, be necessary to reduce the fine below what would otherwise be appropriate if that sum is more than the offender can be fairly required to pay within a reasonable time. The Court of Appeal has suggested (in R v Olliver, 1989) that, although it is common practice to limit financial penalties to what might reasonably be paid over 12 months, a longer period may be appropriate if there are special circumstances which make a heavy fine the best sentence.

5.17   This principle can cause the court problems where the offence is one for which it is usual to impose a fine of a significant amount, but the offender's limited financial resources mean that it would be extremely difficult for him to meet anything more than a very small fine. The offender may, for example, be living on supplementary benefit. The proper course will often be to fine the offender a small amount but to make it clear in passing sentence that this is not an indication that the offence is regarded as trivial but a recognition that even the small fine imposed is a substantial penalty for this particular defendant. Alternatively, the court may consider making a non-financial order. Where immediate punishment is not essential, and the offender may respond to the threat of further punishment on reoffending, a conditional discharge may be an appropriate alternative. Where an immediate punitive sanction does seem called for, a community service order or, (for young offenders) an attendance centre order, might be more suitable – provided that the offence is one punishable with custody. What the the court should not do in these circumstances is to impose a custodial sentence, whether suspended or immediate. If the court's initial assessment is that custody was not required, but a fine would meet the case, it is contrary to established sentencing principles then to substitute a custodial sentence simply because the offender lacks means. To impose a custodial sentence in lieu of a fine under these circumstances has also been deemed to be wrong by the Court of Appeal (in R v McGowan, 1974, and R v Reeves, 1972).

5.18   It is clear from the above discussion that it is necessary for the court to make any enquiry into the offender's means before imposing any financial penalty, not after. It would be quite inappropriate to impose the fine and then to consider means only in the context of considering the arrangements for payment. The law does not require the court to make enquiries, and there will be many cases where the amount of the fine required by the offence is modest and clearly easily within the offender's means. Nevertheless, in most cases it will probably be right to make some pre-fine enquiry as to the offender's income and financial commitments.

Orders to pay the costs of the prosecution
5.19   A defendant who is convicted of an offence may, under the provisions of the Prosecution of Offences Act 1985, be ordered to pay the prosecutor such costs as the court considers just and reasonable. The amount to be paid should be specified in the order.

5.20   The decision whether and to what extent to award costs is entirely within the court's discretion. No firm principles have been laid down, but the following considerations are relevant:

(a) Courts should not make an order to pay prosecution costs unless satisfied that the offender has the means to pay – particularly if also imposing a custodial sentence;

(b) An order for costs may be appropriate when the offender has caused the prosecution to incur unnecessarily heavy costs by contesting a hopeless case. Equally, a guilty plea is a significant consideration in the opposite direction, though a court may in an appropriate case make an award against a defendant who pleaded guilty;

(c) It is, however, wrong to make an order to pay costs simply because the defendant has exercised the right to be tried in the Crown Court for an either way offence. (Nevertheless, if the case is then conducted in a way which makes it justifiable to award costs, those costs will be the higher costs of proceedings in the Crown Court, rather than the

lower costs which would have been incurred in a magistrates'
court);

(d) It will not normally be appropriate to award costs where the offence
is sufficiently trivial only to call for a very small fine (or a non-penal
sentence). Nor may a magistrates' court make an order for costs
against a juvenile which exceeds the amount of any fine
imposed.

Enforcement of financial penalties
5.21 The procedures for enforcing payment by offenders of
compensation, fines, and orders to pay prosecution costs are essentially the
same (though see paragraph 5.32 for some special considerations relating
to compensation orders). Where payment of more than one type of order is
outstanding, a compensation order takes precedence in the enforcement
process over an award of costs, which takes precedence over a fine.

5.22 There are three special categories of case in which the court may on
the occasion of imposing the order commit the offender to prison (or
detention, if the offender is aged 17 to 20) in default of payment. These are
where:

(a) the offence is punishable with imprisonment and the offender
appears to have sufficient money to pay immediately the penalty
imposed for it;

(b) the offender (whatever the offence) is unlikely to remain at an
address in the United Kingdom long enough for the penalty to be
enforced in the normal way;

(c) the offender is being sentenced to custody at the same time, or is
already serving a custodial sentence.

In any of these cases the court may, instead of committing the offender
directly to custody, allow time to pay (by specified instalments, if
appropriate) and either suspend the execution of the order or simply fix a
term to be served in default if the offender fails to pay.

5.23 In any other case, the Crown Court must when imposing a financial
penalty give the offender time to pay but fix a term of custody which the
offender will be ordered to serve in default of payment. The collection and
enforcement of the sum due is then undertaken by the local magistrates'
court, and all the various means of enforcement short of imprisonment, set
out in paragraph 5.27, are available to it.

5.24   Like the Crown Court, a magistrates' court sentencing an offender not in one of the special categories (a) – (c) of paragraph 5.22 must allow time to pay and may order payment by instalments. It may later, on application by or on behalf of the offender, allow further time.

5.25   A fine imposed by a magistrates' court may also be remitted, either in whole or in part, if the court considers at a later hearing that the offender's changed circumstances since conviction – eg loss of employment, serious accident or illness – mean that this would be the just course. The consent of a Crown Court judge must be obtained before remitting a fine imposed by the Crown Court.

5.26   In appropriate cases the court may (either when imposing the order or later) seek to ensure regular payment by making a money payment supervision order. This places the offender under the supervision of a person appointed by the court for as long as some payment is outstanding. Usually the officer nominated for this purpose is a probation officer or ancillary worker.

5.27   Various options are available to a court where it is satisfied that the offender is failing to pay when assets are in fact available to enable payment.

A *Search*
A person may be searched by order of the court, and any money found taken to pay the order, unless the court is satisfied either that the money does not belong to the offender or that the loss of money would be more injurious to the offender's family than would custody in default.

B *Attachment of earnings*
If the offender is in regular employment, the court may consider making an attachment of earnings order. Such an order requires the defaulter's employer to make regular payments from the defaulter's earnings to the clerk to the court. The order served on the employer specifies the total amount to be paid, the 'normal deduction rate' at which the earnings should be applied to paying the fine, and a 'protected earnings rate'. The protected earnings rate is the level below which the court thinks it would not be reasonable to reduce the earnings, and less than normal rate is deducted if the offender's earnings would otherwise fall below the protected earnings rate. If the offender changes his employment, a new order must be made on the new employer, or the order may be redirected to the new employer. A court may make an order of its own initiative if the offender has defaulted, and where attachment of earnings seems an appropriate means of ensuring payment, it may invite the offender to seek

an order when the terms of payment are initially settled. But it is particularly important in the latter case, and should generally be borne in mind, that if there is a possibility of the offender's job being jeopardised, other means of securing payment are normally to be preferred.

C *Distraint of goods*
The court may issue a distress warrant empowering an appointed person (usually a bailiff) to seize a defaulter's property. The property which is seized may then be sold and the proceeds used to pay the fine. The execution of the warrant may also be suspended on conditions, if it is felt that the threat will be sufficient to secure payment. This means of enforcement is frequently used where the defaulter is a limited company, but it may in appropriate cases be used where the defendant is an individual. Certain kinds of property, however, such as goods in a spouse's name or subject to hire purchase agreements, cannot be seized.

5.28 The use of imprisonment or, for young offenders, detention is designed as a sanction of last resort in fine enforcement. Except where the case is one of the special categories mentioned in paragraph 5.22, it is necessary before using it to hold a 'means enquiry', in which an offender in default is required to appear before the court. The offender may also be ordered to provide the court with a statement of means to assist the court's investigation of the financial circumstances. If the original offence was one punishable with imprisonment and the enquiry satisfies the court that the offender has the means to pay the outstanding sum immediately, the offender may be committed to custody whatever the circumstances. Otherwise, however, the court should before issuing a warrant of committal to custody (1) be satisfied that the failure to pay is due to 'wilful refusal or culpable neglect' and (2) have considered or tried other methods of enforcing the payment and either thought them inappropriate or found them unsuccessful.

D *Custody*
5.29 Even if these conditions are satisfied, the court is not bound to issue a warrant with immediate effect. It may, if it considers that the threat constituted by the decision to do so will be enough to produce payment, fix the term of imprisonment or detention but postpone the issue of the warrant on such conditions as it thinks just. This procedure is usually known as a 'suspended warrant of commitment'.

5.30 The maximum period of imprisonment or detention which an offender may be required to serve in default of payment depends on the amount outstanding when the warrant is issued. The maxima apply equally to orders of the Crown Court and the magistrates' courts, and are as follows:

31

Amount not exceeding £50	5 days
Amount exceeding £50 but not exceeding £100	7 days
Amount exceeding £100 but not exceeding £400	14 days
Amount exceeding £400 but not exceeding £1000	30 days
Amount exceeding £1000 but not exceeding £2000	45 days
Amount exceeding £2000 but not exceeding £5000	3 months
Amount exceeding £5000 but not exceeding £10,000	6 months
Amount exceeding £10,000 but not exceeding £20,000	12 months
Amount exceeding £20,000 but not exceeding £50,000	18 months
Amount exceeding £50,000 but not exceeding £100,000	2 years
Amount exceeding £100,000 but not exceeding £250,000	3 years
Amount exceeding £250,000 but not exceeding £1 million	5 years
Amount exceeding £1 million	10 years

Serving the period of custody imposed in default discharges the obligation to pay the outstanding sum, and if part of the term has been served, the sum necessary to secure release from the custody imposed is reduced in the same proportion.

5.31 As paragraph 11.9 explains, enforcement of sums owed by juveniles is subject to rather different arrangements, and the sanction of custody in default is not available. The option of making an attendance centre order on a defaulter is also available (in those areas where there are senior centres) for young adult offenders – ie those aged 17 to 20 – as an alternative to detention. As with imprisonment or detention, an attendance centre order is not purely a means of enforcement, since serving the number of hours imposed extinguishes the offender's liability to the outstanding sum in the same way. (The general limits and arrangements for attendance centre orders imposed in default are the same as those for orders imposed as sentences in their own right, which are described in Chapter 8.) A further special provision applying only to young offenders is that an offender under twenty-one who has been fined by a magistrates' court may not be committed to custody in default unless the court either has previously made a money payment supervision order or is satisfied that it is undesirable or impracticable to do so.

5.32 There are also some distinctive featues in the enforcement of compensation orders. The main difference is that when the Crown Court makes a compensation order, it does not fix the term of imprisonment to be served in the event of default. This is done by the magistrates' court when it deals with the defaulting offender at a means enquiry. The maximum terms which may be fixed are those set out in the table in paragraph 5.30, but if the Crown Court considers that the term provided by this table is insufficient it may make an order imposing a period of over 12 months in default of sums over £20,000 subject to the maxima specified for default in payment of a fine of the same amount. The period which the Crown Court fixes then becomes the maximum period for which the offender may be committed in the event of default; the magistrates' court will then fix the actual term within that maximum. This allows the enforcing court maximum flexibility in seeking to exact payment of the sum due, and reflects the greater emphasis in recovering the money as such, rather than exacting the money as a penalty reflecting the gravity of the offence, when the victim's interests are at stake.

CHAPTER 6

Probation Orders

6.1 Whenever a person aged 17 or over is found guilty of an offence other than one for which the penalty is fixed by law the court may make a probation order if it considers that, having regard to the circumstances, including the nature of the offence and the character of the offender, it is expedient to do so. The minimum period of a probation order is six months and the maximum is three years. A probation order may not be made unless the offender expresses willingness to comply with its requirements.

The aims and methods of probation
6.2 The main aim of a probation order is to bring about an improvement in the offender's behaviour and reduce the incidence of reoffending. When a probation order is made the offender is left at liberty but is subject to certain requirements about his or her way of life, including an obligation to co-operate with the supervising probation officer. The probation officer's skills are used to bring offenders to face up to what they have done, to understand its consequences for others as well as themselves, and to get them to see that they could have avoided offending and can avoid it in the future. The probation service can also help offenders to acquire self-discipline, respect for others and everyday skills (such as how to manage money, how to cook for themselves and how to apply for a job). The probation officer will seek to help the offender with difficulties over money, housing or employment. Special help will be provided for offenders with drug or alcohol problems. Other agencies apart from the probation service may be involved in the programme of supervision.

6.3 Following publication of the Home Office document "Tackling Offending : An Action Plan" in August 1988, almost all of the 56 area probation services have developed a local programme of action to consolidate the best existing practice for the operation of ommunity-based punishments, especially the probation order. Important features of these local action plans are:

34

-   detailed information in social inquiry reports about the way offenders will be supervised

-   feedback to the courts about the progress of offenders individually, or collectively

-   joint working by a number of different agencies to develop programmes of supervision

-   improved monitoring and evaluation of the effectiveness of probation supervision

In some probation areas "intensive probation" programmes are being established which are intended specifically for offenders who would otherwise have received custodial sentences and who may not respond to conventional methods of supervision.

6.4   Because of the ability to assemble different combinations of requirements in a programme adapted to suit the individual offender, the probation order is a very flexible disposal which may be used for a wide range of offenders. In recent years the probation service has devoted increasing resources to supervising the more serious and persistent offenders. Probation orders which are combined with constructive, disciplined and effective programmes of supervision are increasingly being used for offenders who stand to receive custodial sentences.

Offenders for whom probation orders were used in 1988
6.5   Probation orders were made on nearly 44,000 offenders in 1988; 21% of these were females and 26% were over the age of 30. About 42% of the males and 14% of the females had previously experienced a custodial sentence; 12% of the male offenders and 27% of the females had no previous convictions.

The number of people placed on probation in 1988 for the main offences for which the order was used is shown in the following table:

Offence categories	Magistrates' courts		Crown Courts	
	Male	Female	Male	Female
Theft & handling	9,970	4,557	2,671	993
Burglary	3,637	229	2,203	184
Violence against the person	1,882	316	662	198
Fraud & forgery	1,404	963	281	201
Motoring offences (Indictable)	1,476	65	375	13

Requirements

6.6 Every probation order requires the offender to be under the supervision of a probation officer, but the court has power to include in a probation order any other requirement that the court considers necessary for securing his good conduct or preventing him from repeating the offence or committing other offences. If the offender is in need of psychiatric treatment for a mental condition, section 3 of the 1973 Act provides that the order may include a requirement to undergo treatment: this kind of requirement is explained in Chapter 12. There are some restrictions on certain types of requirement. In particular, a probation order may not require the offender to pay monetary compensation for loss, damage or injury caused by his offence. In such cases a compensation order (see Chapter 5) is the appropriate course. A compensation order may be made in addition to a probation order for the same offence. Before making a requirement that the offender should live in a particular place, the court must consider his or her home surroundings. This also applies if a court is considering a requirement of residence in an approved probation hostel.

Approved Probation Hostels

6.7 A requirement of residence in a probation hostel can be for any period not exceeding the term of the probation order. Before including such a requirement, the court must both consider the home surroundings of the offender and establish in advance that a suitable hostel place is available. It is possible to remand a prospective resident to a hostel for a period of 3 to 4 weeks on bail, so providing an opportunity to assess the offender's likely response to the regime. At the end of the period the court can decide, in the light of reports received from the hostel, whether a requirement of residence in a hostel could suitably be imposed. It helps to secure an easier adjustment to life in the outside world if the period of residence is fixed in relation to the duration of the probation order so as to allow the probationer to be under the supervision of a probation officer for about a year beyond the period of the requirement to reside in the hostel. Some residents may be ready to leave before the end of the period of the requirement; in such cases the supervising court has the power to delete or amend the residence requirement.

6.8 There are 81 approved probation hostels, managed by the probation service or voluntary organisations and approved by the Secretary of State. They provide a stable and supportive environment in which groups of up to 40 offenders may learn how to get on with their contemporaries and others, including those in authority. The emphasis is on helping the resident, through group and individual contact both inside and outside the hostel, to move towards a more adequate way of life and away from a pattern of offending. Residents are encouraged to seek normal employment, but where this proves impossible hostels encourage the constructive use of time, including involvement in schemes of work experience, training or education when these are available. Unemployed hostel residents receive benefit from the Department of Social Security from which they are expected to meet the charge levied for their board and lodging, thereby encouraging them to take responsibility for their own affairs.

6.9   Most hostels accept a wide range of age-groups, although a few have a limited age range. Most hostels are for men; some offer places for both sexes, and a smaller number are for women only. Approved probation hostels provide the opportunity for a period of close supervision by hostel staff and probation officers. They are suitable for offenders who have a number of previous convictions, including those who have served periods in custody. Social and emotional inadequacy is likely to be a common factor among these offenders. In many instances offenders will be without home ties or permanent roots in any particular place, and in such cases an important aspect of a hostel's rehabilitation programme will be the recognition and fostering of any ties, however tenuous, which may be developed. Hostel placements, however, are unlikely to be suitable for the most serious offenders or those who by reason of their personal and emotional disturbance or of their addiction to alcohol or drugs need a degree of care or containment which it is not possible to provide in a hostel.

Other specific requirements

6.10   A probation order may require the offender to attend at a particular place at times indicated; if such a requirement is made, the offender must attend, for not more than 60 days, at the place indicated in the order and obey the instructions of the person in charge. Alternatively, the order may require the offender to take part in activities indicated in the order, during the period indicated by the court. In this case, the offender must take part in the activities indicated, as instructed by his probation officer, for not more than 60 days. While doing so, he or she must obey the instructions of the person in charge of the activities.

6.11   These general provisions are intended to make it possible for an offender to take part in a variety of schemes and activities organised by the probation service. The kinds of activities available vary considerably in different parts of the country. There is, however, specific statutory provision for one particular form of activity, the day centre.

6.12 Courts may include in a probation order a requirement that an offender attends a day centre. These are defined as premises at which non-residential facilities are provided for use in connection with the rehabilitation of offenders, and which have been approved by a probation committee for use for persons subject to probation orders. Before including such a requirement, the court must consult a probation officer and satisfy itself that arrangements for attendance can be made and that the person in charge of the centre consents to the inclusion of the requirement for that particular probationer. The maximum period for which attendance may be required is 60 days.

6.13 There are now more than 150 day centres operating in England and Wales which offer a wide variety of facilities. Those recommended for use by the courts as a disposal for more serious offenders will have tough and demanding regimes. Attendance will probably form part of a longer programme of supervision. Day centre staff will work with groups and individuals. Offenders will be made to face up to the consequences of their actions, consider the circumstances of their offending behaviour and the effects it has had on other people. Such day centre programmes will help offenders to make recompense and tackle problems which stand in the way of their becoming law abiding citizens. It is recommended that magistrates visit day centres in their locality to see what kind of programmes are available.

Negative requirements
6.14 Another kind of requirement which is specially mentioned in the law is sometimes called a 'negative requirement' – the court may require the offender to refrain from doing a particular thing during a period of time, provided that it is feasible to secure the offender's compliance.

The use of specific requirements
6.15 If the courts are provided with clear and concise information concerning local probation facilities and the types of offenders for whom they are principally intended, it should be possible for individualised orders and programmes to be devised, based on the use of requirements and/or voluntary understandings.

6.16 None of these requirements may be made unless the court has consulted a probation officer about the offender's circumstances and is satisfied, after that consultation, that 'it is feasible to secure compliance with them'. Imposing requirements which are unenforceable weakens the authority of the courts and does not protect society. The probation order must not include a requirement which would involve the co-operation of someone other than the offender or the probation officer unless the other person consents.

Need for up-to-date local knowledge
6.17   It is important that courts are kept continuously informed of the range of facilities available locally to support probation supervision. The probation liaison committee should make sure that this type of information is readily available to all magistrates, and not only to those who are members of the probation liaison committees. Probation liaison committees also have a duty to 'foster links' between the probation service and the bench, for example by arranging visits to day centres and other facilities provided by the probation service. The probation committee should ensure that judges sitting in their probation area have information about the area probation service and the activities and facilities it provides for offenders. 'Tackling Offending : An Action Plan' placed particular emphasis on the need for good communication between the probation service and sentencers, especially when dealing with the 17–20 year old age group.

Explanation of the effect of the order
6.18   The court must explain to the offender, in ordinary language, the effect of the order generally and in particular the meaning of any additional requirements. He or she must be told that failing to carry out the requirements of the order, or committing another offence, may result in being brought back to court and sentenced for the original offence. The court may not make the order unless the offender indicates willingness to comply with its requirements; and the court must satisfy itself that the offender understands just what is required.

Possible combination with other penalties
6.19   It is possible to combine a probation order with an order to pay the costs of the prosecution or a compensation order. The offender may also be disqualified from driving or recommended for deportation in appropriate circumstances. It is not permissable to fine the offender for the same offence, but if he or she has committed more than one offence, it is possible to make a probation order for one offence and impose a fine for the other.

Effects of a probation order
6.20   As in the case of discharge, the offender is treated by the law as if he

had not been 'convicted' of the offence for most other purposes, unless he is brought back to court after breaking the order or committing another offence and is sentenced in some other way for the original offence. Being placed on probation will, however, disqualify a probationer from jury service for a period of 5 years.

Discharging orders

6.21 The law allows a probation order to be discharged, if either the probation officer or the offender applies to the court. In most cases the court which has authority to discharge the order will be the magistrates' court for the area where the offender lives (the 'supervising court'). If the probation order was made by the Crown Court, the order may be discharged by the supervising court, unless the Crown Court has directed that only the Crown Court may discharge the order. Probation orders may be discharged for good progress or because supervision has proved impracticable; these kinds of discharge usually follow application by the supervising officer. It is also open to a court to substitute an order of conditional discharge.

Proportion of orders successfully completed

6.22 Overall about 80% of probation orders are completed satisfactorily, that is they run their full course, are terminated early for good progress or are replaced by conditional discharge.

6.23 The supervising court may make changes in a probation order, if the probation officer or the offender applies to the court. Existing requirements may be cancelled or new requirements added (provided that the offender is willing to comply with the new requirements). However a requirement that the offender should undergo psychiatric treatment may not be added after the order has been running for more than 3 months. The court may not either shorten or lengthen the period of the probation order in this way: the probation period may be shortened only by discharging it completely, and lengthened only if there is a breach of the order. If there is an application to discharge the probation order, the court may replace it with a conditional discharge for the remainder of the original period of the probation order.

Breach of Probation Orders

6.24 The expression 'breach of probation' is used, often not quite accurately, to describe 2 different happenings – a failure to comply with a requirement of the order or the commission of a further offence during the period of probation. The legal procedures which apply to these 2 cases and the powers of the courts to deal with them are not quite the same, and it is important to distinguish between them.

Failure to comply with the order

6.25 A failure to comply with the requirement of a probation order may happen in many ways, depending on the requirements which the court included in the order. In such cases the supervising probation officer will normally apply to the supervising court for a summons to be issued (in some cases an arrest warrant), and the offender will be brought before the court. The probation officer must prove that the offender has failed to comply with the requirements of the order. In many cases this will be admitted by the offender, but if it is not, the court must hear evidence as in the case of a trial. If the supervising court is satisfied that the offender has failed to comply with the order, it has a number of alternative courses of action. The most important decision which the supervising court must make is whether to allow the probation order to continue or to bring it to an end. If it decides to allow the order to continue, it may either fine the offender up to £400, impose a community service order, or (if the offender is under 21) an attendance centre order. If it does any of these things, the court may also allow the order to continue in effect. Alternatively, the court may decide to terminate the order.

6.26 If the original order was made by a magistrates' court, the supervising court may deal with the offender 'in any manner in which it could deal with him if it had just convicted him of that offence'. This means that the court may pass any sentence which is available for the offence – including a custodial sentence in the form of imprisonment or detention in a young offender institution according to the age of the offender at the time he is brought back to court. (If he was under 21 when he was put on probation, but is now over 21, he must be sentenced as an adult). All the orders which the court may make if it decides to allow the probation order to continue (a fine, a community service order or an attendance centre order) may also be made if the court decides to terminate the order. The court may also make a new probation order for a further period of up to 3 years, if it thinks this is the right course to take.

6.27 If the original probation order was made by the Crown Court, the offender must be sent back to the Crown Court, if the supervising court decided not to deal with the matter in one of the 3 ways which allows the order to continue. When the offender appears before the Crown Court, the probation officer must prove to the satisfaction of the Crown Court that the offender has not complied with the requirements of the order. (The

41

magistrates' court sends a certificate of their finding to the Crown Court; this is not binding on the Crown Court, although it is admissable as evidence.) The Crown Court is then in almost the same position as the supervising court. It may either fine the offender up to £400 or make a community service order, and in either case allow the probation order to continue; or it may terminate the order and sentence the offender for the original offence as if he had just been convicted of that offence before the Crown Court. The sentences which the Crown Court can impose in place of the probation order include a community service order, a fine (although there will be no limit on the amount of the fine) and an attendance centre order if the offender is under 21. The Crown Court may not make an attendance centre order in this case without terminating the probation order. Alternatively, the Crown Court may pass a custodial sentence or make a fresh probation order.

Commission of further offence

6.28 If the offender commits a further offence during the probation period, he may be sentenced for the original offence. The court is not obliged to sentence the offender for the original offence; it may simply allow the probation order to continue for the original period if it considers such a course appropriate.

6.29 If the probation order was made by the Crown Court, only the Crown Court can deal with him. If the order was made by a magistrates' court, he may be dealt with either by the supervising court or by another magistrates' court (if the conviction is before the magistrates' court) with the consent of the supervising court. If the later conviction is before the Crown Court, but the order was made by a magistrates' court, the Crown Court may deal with the original offence, but is limited to sentences which may be passed by a magistrates' court.

6.30 If it is proved to the court's satisfaction that the offender has been convicted of an offence which he committed while on probation, the court may either allow the probation order to continue, or deal with the offender in any manner in which it could have dealt with him if he had just been convicted of the original offence. The court may pass any kind of sentence which would be open to it if there had been no probation order, including a custodial sentence. Whatever sentence is passed, the original probation order comes to an end, although the court can make a fresh probation order for a further period of up to 3 years.

6.31 In 1988 about 8,000 offenders were sentenced for breach (both sorts) of a probation order. The high proportion of custodial sentences reflected

42

the seriousness of the offences for which the orders had originally been made.

Importance of enforcement

6.32   Clearly, there is a relationship between the requirements of orders and breach proceedings. If requirements are too exacting, more breach proceedings are likely to result, with the attendant danger of a greater resort to custody in the long run. To meet this danger it is essential that requirements should make demands that offenders can realistically be expected to fulfil, that there should be high standards in supervisory practice, and that so far as possible a court hearing breach proceedings should be acquainted with the sentencing court's view of the gravity of the offence in respect of which the order was originally made. In the interests of justice, as well as confidence and co-operation between courts and the probation service, it is important that an explicit and consistent policy is applied in the enforcement of probation orders.

CHAPTER 7

Community Service Orders

7.1 Any offender aged 16 or over who is convicted of an offence for which a court can send an adult to prison may be required to perform unpaid work on behalf of the community. An order can only be made with the offender's consent and where suitable work is available. Community service orders must involve a minimum total of 40 hours and a maximum of 240 hours (120 hours for 16 year olds) to be completed within 12 months. The order must specify the petty sessions area in which the offender resides. The work is carried out under the direction of a community service organiser working within the probation service. If for any reason the order is revoked, the offender may be resentenced for the original offence.

7.2 A court making a community service order can in addition make an order for costs, disqualification, compensation or restitution. But the offender may not be fined for the same offence, and he may not be given a suspended sentence of imprisonment for another offence being dealt with at the same time.

Purpose and Use of Community Service

7.3 A community service order represents a substantial deprivation of time: the minimum of 40 hours is 10% more than the maximum 36 hours of a senior attendance centre order; the maximum of 240 hours is 6 times that minimum. The order also involves reparation to the community and a demanding regular commitment. When Parliament accepted the proposal for the introduction of a community service order, it was seen as a penal sanction that made serious demands on the offender. Various judgements of the Court of Appeal have indicated that a community service order can properly be made – if the court is satisfied that the offender is suitable – even for quite serious offences for which the alternative sentence might be a substantial term of imprisonment (see paragraph 7.10).

7.4 National Standards for the operation of community service schemes were brought into force in April 1989 in order to ensure that consistent discipline is maintained in the schemes, and that the orders make real demands on offenders. The standards lay down the type of work to be done by offenders, the way hours worked are reached, standards of performance and behaviour and the action to be taken if an offender fails to comply with the requirements of the order. Detailed information about the Standards is in Home Office Circular 18/1989.

Offenders
7.5 Immediately after its introduction, community service was used predominantly for the 17-20 age group (the order has only been available for 16 year olds since 1983). By 1988 when about 35,000 orders were made, 53% were in respect of the over 21's.

Offences
7.6 The chart set out below shows the main offences in respect of which orders were made by the Crown Court and the magistrates in 1988:

	Number of orders	
	Crown Courts	*Magistrates' Courts*
Theft and handling	3,423	8,836
Burglary	2,602	3,518
Violence	1,514	2,164
Fraud	510	1,189
Motoring offences	539	3,363

Criminal histories of those given community service orders
7.7 Of those offenders sentenced to community service in 1988 about 38% of the males and 17% of the females had previously experienced a custodial sentence. Only 14% of the males and 29% of the females were first offenders.

Before deciding on a community service order
7.8 Before the court makes an order, it must consider a report (and if necessary, hear evidence) from either a probation officer or a social worker about the offender and his circumstances. The court must be satisfied that the offender is a suitable person to do community service. The main criterion is that there must be sufficient stability in the client's living situation for him to be able to maintain commitment to, and complete, a community service order. At certain times, the local scheme may not be able to make provision for offenders with severe personality disorders or severe drink and drug problems, but the feasibility of accepting such

people varies, for instance, with the nature of the tasks available, and it is important that sentencers seek information from the probation service in the offender's home area. Arrangements can be made for those who live in Scotland or Northern Ireland and are convicted by courts in England and Wales to do community service under the schemes which operate in those jurisdictions, although arrangements for 16 year olds are not available in Northern Ireland.

Need to indicate basis of inquiries

7.9   When adjourning for a social inquiry report to assess an offender's suitability for community service, a court needs to make clear what it has in mind. The Court of Appeal has stated that if a court adjourns sentence to enable an offender's fitness for a particular non-custodial measure to be assessed, it is bound to impose that measure if a favourable assessment is received. Therefore if a court wishes to keep its options open, the request for a report must be clearly stated to be on a 'without prejudice' basis.

7.10   Having reached its decision, the court must explain to the offender that the order requires him to report to the relevant officer and perform, for the number of hours specified, such work at such times as may be instructed by the officer. There is also an obligation for an offender to notify the officer of any change of address. Additionally, the court must inform the offender what may happen to him if he fails to carry out the requirements of the order and the fact that the court may review the order on the application of either himself or the probation officer. Copies of the order must then be passed to the probation officer forthwith, as he has the responsibility of serving a copy on the offender and delay can invalidate the order.

Length of community service orders

7.11   The social inquiry report will include mention of factors relating to the offender or his circumstances which will influence his ability to complete orders of a particular length within a 12 month period. Because of the differences between offenders, there is no clearly established tariff for length of orders. The Court of Appeal has given guidance by suggesting 190 hours for burglary meriting 9-12 months' imprisonment. It is important for the court to consider whether the community service order is being made as an alternative to a custodial sentence. If it is not, then this fact should be recorded in the court register (see paragraph 7.22 below). The Lord Chief Justice has said that if the alternative would not have been a custodial sentence, the order should be for a small number of hours only.

7.12 A court dealing on one occasion with 2 or more offences may make a comparable number of community service orders to run concurrently or consecutively. It is feasible in such a case for consecutive orders to be of less than 40 hours so long as the aggregate reaches the minimum of 40 hours. The maximum must not exceed 240 hours (120 hours for a 16 year old). If a court is sentencing an offender already subject to a community service order made on another occasion, it may make a consecutive order but not one such that the permissible maximum is exceeded.

7.13 If an offender has spent time in custody on remand, and the court decides to make a community service order, the Court of Appeal has decided that, in recognition of the time in custody, it is reasonable for the length of the order to be reduced.

The operation of community service
7.14 Community service work is usually done in spells of several hours on one day a week. When relatively few offenders were unemployed, almost all the work was undertaken at weekends. This is no longer the case, and most schemes can provide work on any day of the week. Should an offender have a job, his community service will be arranged accordingly, and work would not be arranged that conflicted with his religious beliefs or education. The necessity for frequent, punctual reporting is part of the discipline imposed by the order.

7.15 The sort of work which is available varies widely at different times of the year and from one part of the country to another. However, all offenders who are serving orders of 60 hours or more must spend 21 hours with a group of offenders performing some type of manual work. Direction of the work may be by a local voluntary or public body (with the guidance and support of the probation service organiser) or by supervisors employed by the probation service. All work is unpaid and of a sort normally undertaken by voluntary effort; some tasks involve offenders working alongside volunteers. The extent to which tasks involve contact with beneficiaries varies widely: helping in outdoor conservation projects, building adventure playgrounds, repairing toys for children in need, painting and decorating houses and flats for the elderly and handicapped are examples of tasks at one end of the spectrum. At the other are tasks which involve close personal contact such as swimming coaching for handicapped children, visiting and helping the elderly and helping at disabled people's sports clubs. Should an offender have particular skills or aptitudes, it may well be possible for these to be used.

7.16 Offenders made subject to community service orders are given the opportunity to make amends to the community for some of the harm they have done. This reparative element is common to all orders. For some offenders there will be rehabilitative effects. To be a 'giver' rather than a 'taker' may be a novel and maturing experience; some offenders may thus be helped to see themselves and their place in the community in a different light. There have been many heartening examples of offenders reformed by their community service experience but, as with all human reactions, the likelihood of this happening cannot be predicted in respect of any particular offence.

7.17   The decision as to placement is made by the community service organiser, not the court. It is, however, obviously desirable for sentencers to be aware of developments in their local schemes and to keep in close touch with the community service organiser. Under the National Standards for community service orders, the magistrates or judge responsible for making a community service order should be notified of its successful completion or reasons for termination before completion. Information on this and other aspects of local schemes is available from the local probation service; they will also be pleased to arrange visits by small groups of sentencers to observe the operation of schemes.

7.18   Once it has been made, a community service order remains in force until the specified hours are completed or the order is ended by a court. If the hours have not been completed within 12 months for some reason such as the offender's illness, the order may be extended by a magistrates' court acting for the area specified in the order, on the application of the offender or the probation officer. If, however, the specified hours are not going to be completed, there are 2 courses of action open to a court; breach proceedings (explained in paragraphs 7.19 – 7.21) and revocation (paragraphs 7.22 – 7.26).

Breach and revocation of community service orders
7.19   If an offender has failed to carry out the order, by not notifying a change of address, not going to the place where he is told to do the work or not working satisfactorily when he is there or sufficiently frequent to complete the order within the time allowed, the community service organiser may apply for a summons or warrant, and the offender is brought before the court. The National Standards for community service orders lay down a strict policy on breach which each area probation service is expected to follow. When he appears, the community service organiser must prove to the satisfaction of the court that the offender has failed to carry out the order 'without reasonable excuse'. If the offender does not admit this, the allegations must be proved by calling evidence as in a trial. If the magistrates' court is satisfied that the offender has failed to

comply with a community service order which was made by a magistrates' court, it may either: order the offender to pay a fine of up to £400, and let the order remain in force; or revoke the order, and sentence the offender for the original offence in any way in which he could have been sentenced by the court which made the order in the first place, making due allowance for any hours which have been worked.

7.20   If the community service order was made by the Crown Court, the magistrates' court may order the offender to pay a fine of up to £400 and allow the order to remain in force or commit him to the Crown Court. If the offender is committed, the Crown Court must hear the evidence again; if the Crown Court is satisfied that the allegations have been proved, it may fine the offender up to £400 and allow the order to continue or bring it to an end and pass any sentence on the offender which it could have passed when it originally made the order.

7.21   When a breach has been proved, the community service organiser can be invited to advise on the prospect of the order being successfully completed. The bringing of breach proceedings may be a positive enforcement measure which stimulates the offender to a better response, and the order can then be successfully completed. On the other hand, if experience has shown that there is no reasonable prospect of the order being completed, the most appropriate action would be to terminate it.

7.22   In 1988, 8,250 people were dealt with by the courts for failing to carry out the requirements of the community service order; about 350 of these were females. The chart below shows the number of males given various sentences for the original offence following revocation for breach of requirements:-

	Magistrates' Courts	Crown Courts
Conditional discharge	96	37
Probation order	293	117
Fine	3,483	209
Young Offender Institution	679	715
Imprisonment	470	651
Otherwise dealt with	677	471
TOTAL	5,698	2,200

The orders of those otherwise dealt with were mostly revoked without sentence or allowed to continue. The high proportion of custodial sentences emphasises the importance of the point mentioned in paragraph 7.11 above, of noting when the order is made if it is not being used as a substitute for custody.

7.23   A magistrates' court may be asked to review an order because of some change in an offender's circumstances which makes completion impracticable – for instance, a substantial prison sentence or the acquisition of exceptionally heavy family responsibilities. If the court is satisfied that it would be in the interest of justice to do so, it may revoke the order, passing an alternative sentence or making an order. If the order was made by the Crown Court, the offender must be committed for revocation to that Court.

7.24   Reoffending during the currency of a community service order is not itself a breach of the order – the position is not the same as under a probation order or a suspended sentence. However, the outcome of the proceedings for the later offence may mean that the offender is no longer able to carry out the community service order – particularly if he is given a custodial sentence for the later offence. The law makes different provisions according to whether the later offence is dealt with by the magistrates' court or Crown Court.

7.25   If the later offence is dealt with by the magistrates' court, the court may not interfere with the community service order unless it passes a custodial sentence for the new offence. If it does pass a custodial sentence for the later offence, and either the offender or the community service organiser applies to do so (and the original community service order was made by a magistrates' court), the court may revoke the order (if it considers it to be in the interests of justice to do so) but cannot re-sentence for the original offence. If the community service order was made by the Crown Court, the magistrates' court must commit the offender to the Crown Court. The Crown Court may revoke the order but also cannot re-sentence.

7.26   If the later offence is dealt with by the Crown Court, the Court may (if it seems to be in the interest of justice to do so) either revoke the order or revoke the order and sentence the offender to any kind of sentence which would have been passed on him by the court which made the community service order. The Crown Court can take this step on its own initiative, without waiting for an application by the offender or the community service organiser.

7.27   Because of the practical difficulties in getting an offender produced from custody for revocation proceedings, it is highly desirable that the question of revocation should be considered when a custodial sentence is imposed. The essential question is 'Can the community service order still be completed within the 12 month period?' If this is unlikely to be feasible, then revocation at the time the custodial sentence is imposed is the desirable course.

CHAPTER 8

Attendance Centre Orders

8.1   Anyone aged under twenty-one who is found guilty of an offence for which an adult may be imprisoned may be ordered to attend at an attendance centre for a number of hours. An attendance centre order may also be made where the offender has not complied with another order (eg default in paying a fine; breach of a supervision order or a probation order requirement). The maximum total number of hours is thirty-six, or twenty-four if the offender is aged under 17. The minimum is twelve hours (though where the offender is aged under 14 the court has discretion to impose less). The order is served by attending the attendance centre on several different occasions – the longest period for which an offender can be required to attend on any one day is three hours.

8.2   The aims of the order are to impose, in loss of leisure over a considerable period, a punishment that is generally understood by young people and to encourage them, in a disciplined environment, to make more constructive use of their leisure time. The sentence will not normally be suitable for those who have a long record of offences or who need removal from bad home surroundings, nor can it, of itself, meet a requirement for sustained supervision. It can, however, be ordered as an alternative to custody for an offence of some gravity. A court may make a further attendance centre order on an offender already serving one, but may not make an order on an offender who has previously received a custodial sentence unless this is warranted by special circumstances.

8.3   The Home Office is responsible for providing attendance centres, but they are a locally based provision, being run in the vast majority of cases by police officers. There are over 100 attendance centres, most of which cater for boys aged 10 – 16, but in some of the larger towns there are also mixed junior centres for boys and girls of the same age group and several senior centres which take boys aged 17 – 20. An Order cannot be made on an offender unless a centre is available in the area for offenders of the relevant sex and age group. Since repeated attendance is required, the court must also be satisfied that the offender can get to the centre reasonably easily.

Where an offender is not normally resident in the area served by the court, an order may be made to take effect in the offender's home area (if a suitable centre is available).

8.4 The centres themselves are wherever possible situated in school buildings equipped with a gymnasium and showers; other locations include youth clubs; police premises out of sight of the public and community centres. Centres run by the police have civilians on their staff as well as police instructors, and vice versa. Sessions are held on Saturdays, at most centres in the afternoon. They normally last two hours at junior centres and three hours at senior centres. One part of each session is devoted to physical training and the remaining time to constructive leisure activity: for example craftwork or instruction on topics such as citizenship and first aid. Officers in charge of centres have discretion to develop the regime to suit the local conditions and the needs and aptitudes of the offenders sent to them.

8.5 Either the offender or the officer in charge of the centre may apply to the court to discharge the order. An offender who fails to attend at the times when he has been ordered to do so or who breaks the rules of the centre in a manner which the officer in charge cannot adequately deal with may be brought before the magistrates' court. If the failure to attend or the grave misconduct is proved to the court's satisfaction, it may deal with him in any way open to it in sentencing for the original offence, including custody, (or, if the order was made by the Crown Court, commit the offender to be dealt with by that Court). The fresh order made in these circumstances should have regard to the gravity of the initial offence; the seriousness of the failure to comply with the court order; the necessary discipline of the attendance centre and the proportion of the order properly served.

CHAPTER 9

Imprisonment

The Use of Imprisonment

9.1 Imprisonment is the most severe penalty ordinarily available to the courts. It is also by far the most expensive. (See *Appendix 3*). Only offenders aged 21 and over may be sent to prison – the various custodial sentences which may be imposed on younger offenders are discussed in *Chapter 10*. Imprisonment is intended as a deterrent and as a punishment. As Paragraph 3.7 explains, experience indicates that imprisonment is unlikely to lead to the reform of many offenders. On the contrary, particularly with less experienced offenders, it may merely teach them how to be better criminals. The Court of Appeal has suggested that imprisonment should be regarded as a sanction of the last resort reserved for the more serious and violent offender, and this should always be taken into account by the court. A prison sentence should not be imposed solely with rehabilitative aims in mind. Prison regimes are designed to take constructive steps to prepare offenders for law-abiding behaviour on release. However, these are limited by the available resources and the need to maintain proper security and discipline. The non-custodial options available to the Courts should always be considered first unless a non-custodial penalty would be wholly inappropriate. In R v Stewart (1987), for example, the Court of Appeal made it clear that for non-violent offences, such as welfare benefit fraud, courts should consider carefully whether a custodial sentence was necessary or whether a non-custodial penalty, such as community service, might be suitable.

9.2 The fact that the penalty of imprisonment is available for an offence does not mean that it will always – or, for most offences, usually – be necessary to impose imprisonment on defendants convicted of it. The maximum sentence of imprisonment is intended to reflect the gravity of the worst examples of that offence. Apart from the special case of murder, which carries a mandatory penalty of life imprisonment, all imprisonable offences may alternatively be dealt with by any of the non-custodial measures discussed in *Chapters 4 – 7*. For some offences – such as causing death by reckless driving (see paragraph 3.8) – the Court of Appeal has given clear guidance on the kinds of aggravating factors likely to warrant imprisonment. Many common crimes are offences, triable either way, which can vary greatly in gravity. Examples are theft, burglary and assault occasioning actual bodily harm. Clearly the least serious cases, including most of those dealt with in the magistrates' courts, will not warrant a sentence of imprisonment. Many factors will be relevant to the decision – for example, the degree of premeditation; the injury caused or value of property involved; the offender's record and attitude to the offence; the use or carrying of an offensive weapon. There are no set rules for weighing up these factors and deciding whether a particular case is serious enough to justify imprisonment. The facts of each case and the circumstances of every offender should be considered individually by the court, taking into account any guidance issued by the Court of Appeal. The figures in *Appendix 2* indicate, for the main broad categories of offences, the use made by the Courts of the various penalties. More detailed statistics are published each year by HMSO in "Criminal Statistics".

9.3   Once the court has decided that the offence being heard is sufficiently serious to merit a prison sentence, there are a number of points which must be considered by the court. These are: the length of the sentence, suspending or partly suspending the sentence and the rules governing release from prison.

The length of prison sentences

Statutory limits
9.4   The power of the court to impose a sentence of imprisonment is usually subject to a maximum term given by the Act of Parliament which creates the particular offence concerned. The maximum term is intended as an indication of the penalty appropriate for the worst possible case of it. For the major crimes the maximum terms are thus very high – eg life imprisonment for rape, robbery or manslaughter; 14 years for burglary; 10 years for theft. Most prison terms imposed, however, are far below the maximum because the offending falls well below the order of gravity which the maximum is designed to cater for. The precedents established for most common offences by the Court of Appeal over the years are a more useful guide to the range of penalties imposed for serious cases, heard in the Crown Court, where various aggravating factors are present.

9.5   Magistrates' courts, as was noted in paragraph 2.3 are generally limited in their sentencing powers, and a magistrates' court may not impose more than six months' imprisonment for any offence. Nor may they impose a term shorter than five days.

Consecutive and concurrent terms

9.6   An offender may be sentenced at one time for several offences, and the court may consider that imprisonment is the right penalty to impose for more than one of them. It may order that the various prison sentences are to run concurrently (so that in effect the offender serves a single sentence no longer than the greatest individual term which has been passed) or consecutively (so that each individual sentence is served in turn, and the overall term is thus prolonged), or in some combination of the two. The courts have developed two general principles governing the decision whether to impose consecutive or concurrent terms. The first is that consecutive sentences should not be passed for different offences arising out of the same transaction or series of acts. If the offender commits what is essentially one criminal action, but which gives rise to a number of associated criminal charges, the sentence for those offences should normally be ordered to run concurrently. The second principle, often referred to as 'the totality principle', is that whenever a court imposes consecutive sentences, it should always ensure that the total combined sentence is not excessive or unjust in relation to the types of offence committed or unsuitable for the offender. If the total is excessive (whatever the merits of the individual sentences for the particular offences) the court should make some reduction in the overall effective term. (A similar principle applies to multiple fines – see paragraph 5.15.)

9.7   Magistrates' courts may in some circumstances pass consecutive sentences imposing an effective overall prison term of over six months. If the court is sentencing for more than one offence triable either way, it may impose consecutive terms for those offences up to a maximum of twelve months. It may also order that any suspended prison terms previously imposed on the offender, of which he is in breach, take effect consecutively to any terms it may order for the offences of which he currently stands convicted.

General Court of Appeal Guidance

9.8   The Court of Appeal has stated that sentencers must be particularly careful to examine each case in which custody is necessary to ensure that the term imposed is as short as possible, consistent with the courts' duty to protect the interests of the public and to punish and deter the criminal. The court could, and should ask itself whether there was any compelling reason why a short sentence should not be passed. This principle applies throughout the range of custodial sentences: a very short term might suffice where what was primarily required was to demonstrate that the offence demanded the punishment of custody; the Crown Court might also feel, in dealing with more serious cases, that many offenders might as justly and effectively be dealt with by a sentence of six or nine months as by one of eighteen months or three years. The extent to which it was possible to pass shorter sentences would naturally depend on the importance of deterrence in dealing with the particular type of offence. As general illustrations, the Court mentioned (in the 1980 case of Bibi) that the case for shorter sentences applied to the less serious type of factory-breaking or shop-breaking rather than to burglary of private homes; to petty frauds involving small amounts of money rather than to planned crime for wholesale profit; to minor cases of sexual indecency rather than to robbery or serious violence (such as the use of a weapon to wound) and to fringe participants in serious crimes rather than to its instigators. This general reference to broad categories of crime was not, however, intended to deny the importance of considering the circumstances of the individual offender and the individual offence. The aim was uniformity of approach, not uniformity of sentence.

9.9 Also specified in the Bibi judgement was a particular class of defendant – the first offender, for whom any prison sentence, however short, might be a sufficient punishment and deterrent. As has been mentioned (in *Chapter 3*), there are particular procedural safeguards operating to ensure that particular care is taken in sentencing an offender to prison for the first time: legal representation; a social inquiry report and stated reasons why the court considers no alternative sentence appropriate will all normally be required. But for certain kinds of offender being imprisoned for the first time it may also be right to make the length of any unavoidable prison sentence as short as possible. The type of offender concerned is usually middle-aged and of blameless previous character; the offences often (but not invariably) offences of dishonesty committed against an employer, or some other person to whom the offender owed a particular responsibility. This principle has been endorsed by the Court of Appeal (for instance in the 1980 case of R v Jones). Offenders of this type fall within the 'clang of the prison gates' principle, in the sense that a very short sentence may be sufficient penalty and deterrent, because the very fact of imprisonment is the real punishment.

Suspended sentences
9.10 Where the court decides that the offence, seen in the light of the offender's record, is sufficiently serious to justify a sentence of imprisonment of not more that two years, it should proceed to consider whether the operation of that sentence may be fully suspended. A sentence within this range may be suspended for a period (known as the 'operational period') of at least one year and not more than two years. The suspended prison term is not served at all unless the offender commits a further imprisonable offence during the operational period.

9.11   In deciding that it may properly suspend a prison sentence on a particular offender, a court may consider whether the threat of activating it is likely to be effective in deterring the offender from further criminal activity during the operational period. The court should not, however, pass a suspended sentence simply in order to achieve this effect if the offence itself is not sufficiently serious to justify a prison sentence. Parliament has stated that a court should not pass a suspended sentence unless an immediate prison sentence would have been appropriate in the absence of the power to suspend it. It follows that it is also wrong to pass a suspended sentence for an offence for which most offenders would be fined, simply because the particular offender does not have the money to pay a fine (as was also mentioned in paragraph 5.17). Moreover, the fact that a prison sentence is to be suspended should make no difference to what would otherwise be its appropriate length. The decision on the appropriate length should come before the decision whether the sentence may be suspended.

9.12   There is no necessary link between the length of the suspended prison term, which will primarily depend on the gravity of the offence, and the length of the operational period, which will have regard to the circumstances of the offender. It is possible to have a short sentence (say three months) suspended for two years or a longer sentence (say two years) suspended for twelve months.

9.13   A court which passes a fully suspended sentence may not make a probation order at the same time (even as a separate sentence for a different charge dealt with on the same occasion). If the Crown Court feels that the offender needs help from a probation officer, and the sentence is one of more than six months, it may add to the sentence a suspended sentence supervision order. Such an order lasts for a period specified by the court which must not exceed the operational period of the suspended sentence. Unlike a probation order, it does not require the consent of the offender. During the specified period the offender is under the supervision of a probation officer, and must keep in touch with that officer and in particular notify any change of address. The order may not include any other requirements (by contrast with the probation order). An offender who fails to comply may be brought before a magistrates' court and fined up to £400 if found in breach of the order. The offender is not, however, thereby also liable to activation of the suspended sentence, which can only happen if a further imprisonable offence is committed during the operational period. A court making a suspended sentence supervision order must explain its meaning to the offender in ordinary language.

9.14   An offender found guilty of a further imprisonable offence committed during the operational period of a suspended sentence must be dealt with for the breach of the suspended sentence by a court which has the authority to do so. A magistrates' court may only do so where the original suspended sentence was passed by a magistrates' court. Where the original suspended sentence was passed by the Crown Court, it should commit the offender to the Crown Court for breach of its suspended sentence to be dealt with (and the Crown Court may also there deal with any offence of which the magistrates have summarily convicted the offender in finding him in breach).

9.15 The first task of the court dealing with the breach of the suspended sentence should be to decide what sentence best corresponds to the gravity, in its own right, of the latest offence. If the court decides on a probation order or a discharge, the proceedings do not count as a conviction for the purpose of the operation of the suspended sentence, and the question what action to take for the breach accordingly does not arise. Otherwise, the offender must be dealt with for the suspended sentence, and the court must order that the suspended sentence take effect in full, in addition to any punishment imposed for the subsequent offence, unless it is of the opinion that it would be unjust to do so in view of all the circumstances, including the facts of the subsequent offence. If it is of that opinion, it must state its reason, and may then take one of three other courses: (a) order the sentence to take effect with a shorter term; (b) extend the operational period by up to a further two years; (c) 'make no order', which means that the offender cannot be dealt with again for the suspended sentence unless he is convicted of a further imprisonable offence committed within the original operational period. (It is important for the court to make it clear that it has chosen this course, and what the effect of that decision is.) The main factor which might justify not activating the suspended sentence in full is the triviality of the later offence, either absolutely or by comparison with the original one. The court dealing with the breach cannot, however, seek to assess the merits of the suspended sentence originally imposed. Some credit may also be given, usually in the form of a reduction in the term of the suspended sentence, where the later offence was committed close to the end of the operational period.

9.16 If the suspended sentence is activated (wholly or in part) and the offender is also sentenced to immediate imprisonment for the subsequent offence, it is normally good practice to order the terms to be consecutive rather than concurrent, thereby representing the additional misconduct involved in the breach of the court's original terms of suspension. The court must always, however, have regard to the totality principle (see paragraph 9.6). If the court imposes a prison sentence, it should also ensure that the overall sentence is not such as to leave an outstanding liability once the offender has been discharged from prison. It would in particular be wrong to impose an immediate prison sentence for the latest offence and leave the suspended sentence in operation, or extend it, so that it remains operative on the offender's release, or to achieve the same effect by imposing a suspended sentence for the latest offence.

Partly suspended sentences

9.17 A court may decide that an offence is so serious that it merits a prison term of between three months and two years and it would not be right to suspend the sentence fully (or to substitute for it a substantial community service order). It should consider whether the circumstances of the particular offender are such that the immediate serving of part of the sentence and the suspension of the remainder is sufficient both to punish and to deter for the future. If the court considers it appropriate to mitigate the full impact of the prison sentence in this way, it may pass a partly suspended prison sentence, specifying what portion is to be served immediately and what to be suspended. The portion to be served immediately must be at least 28 days, but may not be more than three-quarters of the 'whole term' of the sentence (ie that pronounced by the court, without any allowance for remission or parole). The 'operational period' of the suspended portion is not, as with the fully suspended sentence, a matter to be separately decided by the court. It is the time between the offender's release from the immediate portion of the sentence and the end of the whole term.

9.18 If a partly suspended sentence is passed, the court may not make a probation order at the same time (even if the offender is before the court on several charges), and there is no power to make a supervision order, as there is in the case of fully suspended sentences of more than six months. It is possible to make a number of partly suspended sentences run consecutively, but the Court of Appeal has said that the correct practice is to treat the combined total sentence as a single sentence and to make a single order for partial suspension in relation to the whole term (provided that it does not exceed two years).

9.19 The Court of Appeal has also stressed that great care should be taken to ensure that the power of partial suspension is not used in any way which might serve to increase the length of the sentence. In many cases, of which first-time offenders were the most obvious examples, a short term of immediate imprisonment was a sufficient shock, without any additional suspended period. The partial suspension power is especially applicable to serious first-time offenders, or first-time prisoners, and possibly to those whose last term of imprisonment was some time ago. In cases where something more than a short sentence is required to mark public disapproval of the crime, and as a deterrent, individual mitigation for offenders of this kind can appropriately be recognised by partial suspension.

9.20 Both fully and partly suspended sentences are sentences of imprisonment for the purposes of all the provisions of the law relating to such sentences, and in particular those provisions specifying various requirements to be fulfilled before a prison sentence may be imposed. A partly suspended sentence counts for most purposes as a single sentence for the whole term, though for the purposes of the rules governing early release from prison terms (summarised in the following paragraphs) the immediate portion and the suspended portion, if it should be activated, are treated as separate sentences.

9.21 An offender convicted of an offence punishable with imprisonment during the suspended portion of a partly suspended sentence (having been released from the immediate term), may be brought before a court having authority to deal with the matter. (As with breach of fully suspended sentences, a magistrates' court may only deal with sentences imposed by magistrates' courts). The court may order the offender to serve the whole of the suspended term. If it considers it unjust to do so, in view of all the circumstances, including the facts of the later offence, it may instead order that only a part of the suspended portion be now served or make no order. If it decides to make no order, it must give reasons for that decision.

Parole and Remission
9.22 It is not the practice of the courts when imposing a prison sentence to consider the possibility of release before the full term of the sentence through the operation of the provisions relating to remission or parole. The sentence passed by the court defines the limit of the offender's liability to punishment; earlier release results from the exercise of executive powers governed by statutory rules. Parole and remission are nevertheless an important part of the context of the operation both of the partly suspended sentence (described in paragraphs 9.17 – 9.18) and, more particularly, of the special arrangements implied by the extended sentence and the life sentence (described in paragraphs 9.26 – 9.29). The following paragraphs accordingly briefly summarise the rules governing early release from ordinary determinate prison sentences.

9.23 Subject to good behaviour in prison, the rules allow for remission of normally one-half of a sentence imposed by the Court when that sentence is more than 5 days, but does not exceed 12 months, and remission of one-third for longer sentences. But when a sentence is served consecutively as part of a total term exceeding 12 months, irrespective of whether, if when it was first imposed, the offender was entitled to half-remission, that sentence will attract a maximum of one-third remission. This means that in practice any prisoner will be released after serving one-half or two-thirds of the total term imposed, depending on its length, unless he has been ordered to forfeit a specified amount of remission by a prison disciplinary body.

9.24 Parole is, on the other hand, a discretionary and conditional system of release. It applies only to prisoners who:

(a) have served at least one third of the terms imposed by the court; and

(b) have served at least six months in prison from the date of sentence; and

(c) have been recommended for release by the Parole Board (or the Local Review Committee at the prison) and approved for release by the Home Secretary.

The combined effect of (a) and (b) and the dual remission rate is to confine the possibility of release on parole to prisoners serving terms of over twelve months. Prisoners released on parole are on licence, and thereby subject to supervision and to possible recall to serve the remainder of the sentence, until the date on which they would otherwise have been released – that is, normally, until two-thirds of the term imposed by the court has elapsed. The decision whether to release a particular prisoner takes account of the offence, the offender's prospects on release and the offender's conduct in prison.

9.25 If the offender has spent time in police custody or in prison on remand before being sentenced to prison, that time is normally counted towards the sentence (except for any days that the offender was at the same time in custody as a sentenced prisoner, including for non-payment of a fine or other payment ordered by a court, or for contempt). This pre-sentence custody time counts for the purpose of calculating remission of sentence. It does not, however, count towards the six months' minimum period which must be served before an offender may be considered for parole. Nor does such a period before a (fully) suspended sentence is imposed, or before a probation order, community service order or order for conditional discharge is made, count towards any term subsequently imposed with the activation of the suspended sentence or for breach of the order.

Extended Sentences

9.26　The extended sentence (which is now rarely used) is a form of prison sentence which may be passed on persistent offenders. It differs from an ordinary prison sentence in that (a) the court may in some cases impose a term in excess of the maximum for the offence and (b) there is no entitlement to remission of sentence. If the offender is released on parole he is subject to supervision and recall until the end of the whole term imposed by the court. The purpose is to protect the public for a substantial time from an offender who has shown 'by reason of his previous conduct and of the likelihood of his committing further offences' the need for such a course. This may justify a sentence which would be too severe if passed as a normal sentence, and supervision within the community after release for a longer period than would normally be appropriate. There is no obligation to pass an extended sentence of any particular length, but if the normal maximum for the offence is less than five years, an extended sentence of up to five years may be passed and if the normal maximum is from five to ten years an extended sentence of up to ten years may be passed. (For offences with normal maxima of ten years or more, the extended sentence may not exceed the normal maximum).

9.27　Extended sentences may be passed only on offenders who:

(a) have committed the latest offence within three years of a previous conviction for an offence punishable with (at least) two years' imprisonment or of being released from a prison sentence imposed for such an offence; and

(b) have been convicted by the Crown Court on at least three previous occasions since the age of twenty-one of offences punishable with two years' imprisonment; and

(c) have been sentenced on those occasions to a total of at least five years' imprisonment; and

(d) have on at least two occasions been sentenced to terms of imprisonment for an offence and either one was for three years or more or two were for two years or more.

Life Imprisonment

9.28　A life sentence is wholly indeterminate. There is no remission, nor do the normal parole arrangements apply, and there is no entitlement to release at any stage. Equally, the offender may be considered for release on licence at any stage, and there is no requirement to serve any specified minimum period. Release may only be authorised by the Home Secretary, on the recommendation of the Parole Board and after consulting the Lord

Chief Justice and the trial judge (if available). A prisoner released from a life sentence remains on licence for the rest of his life, and may be recalled to prison at any time by the Home Secretary or the Parole Board. (The licence may also be revoked by the Crown Court if it convicts him of a further imprisonable offence).

9.29   Life imprisonment must be imposed on all persons aged 21 and over convicted of murder. In passing this mandatory life sentence the court may, if it wishes, recommend that the offender should not be released until he has served a specified minimum number of years in prison. Although such recommendations weigh heavily with the Parole Board and the Home Secretary, they are not binding on them; nor do they in any way guarantee release as soon as that term has been served. Life imprisonment is also the maximum sentence which a court may pass for a number of the gravest crimes, including manslaughter; robbery; rape; buggery; wounding with intent to do grievous bodily harm; aggravated burglary and certain firearms offences. For these offences, the court may choose instead to impose determinate prison terms of any length, or a non-custodial penalty. The Court of Appeal has suggested that the life sentence for these offences will normally be appropriate only where the court concludes, usually after considering medical evidence, that the offender is dangerous, and likely to commit grave offences in the future if prematurely released. The life sentence allows any eventual release of such an offender to be determined in the light of observation of the offender's subsequent behaviour, and any maturation, during the sentence, with public safety considerations paramount. The life sentence should not be used simply because an offence was particularly heinous, when a long determinate sentence would be more appropriate.

CHAPTER 10

Custodial Penalties for Young Offenders

10.1   In considering young offenders it is helpful to divide them into two groups: 'juveniles' (ie those aged under 17) and 'young adults' (ie those aged 17 and under 21). For many purposes the treatment of juvenile offenders needs to be considered separately (see *Chapter 11*). However, no offender aged under 21 may be sentenced to imprisonment, and the sentence of detention in a young offender institution (which is the main custodial sentence for young offenders) is available for both juveniles and young adults. It is thus convenient to discuss the use and availability of the various forms of custody for young offenders as a whole. This chapter describes the sentences available and the circumstances in which they may be imposed.

10.2   The basic principle that custody must be used only as a last resort applies with particular force to young offenders. Section 1 of the Criminal Justice Act 1982 (as amended by section 123 of the Criminal Justice Act 1988) gives statutory effect to this principle. Section 1(4) provides that a sentence of detention in a young offender institution (see paragraph 10.5) or a sentence of custody for life (see paragraph 10.12) may not be passed unless the court is satisfied:

(i)   that the circumstances, including the nature and gravity of the offence, are such that if the offender were aged 21 or over the court would pass a sentence of imprisonment; and

(ii)   that the offender qualifies for a custodial sentence.

Section 1(4A) sets out the criteria for qualification for a custodial sentence. These are that:

(a)   the offender has a history of failure to respond to non-custodial penalties and is unable or unwilling to respond to them; or

(b)   only a custodial sentence would be adequate to protect the public from serious harm from him; or

(c)   his offence was so serious that a non-custodial sentence for it cannot be justified.

64

10.3   Section 2 of the 1982 Act requires courts to obtain a social inquiry report before imposing a sentence of detention in a young offender institution or of custody for life to see whether there is a more appropriate way of dealing with the young offender. There is an exception to this requirement if, in the circumstances, the court thinks that it is necessary to obtain a social inquiry report. Section 2(4) of the 1982 Act (as amended by section 123(5) of the 1988 Act) requires a court passing a sentence of detention in a young offender institution or of custody for life to state in open court

(a) that it is satisfied that the offender qualifies for a custodial sentence; and

(b) which of the criteria in section 1 (4A) is relevant; and

(c) the reasons why it thinks the criterion is met.

The court must also explain to the offender in ordinary language in open Court why it is passing a custodial sentence on him.

10.4   As the Court of Appeal has held in many cases, the youth of an offender may be a factor justifying a shorter term of custody than might be necessary for a more mature and hardened criminal. Whatever term is imposed, a custodial sentence on a young offender may not be wholly or partly suspended.

Detention in a Young Offender Institution
10.5   The sentence of detention in a young offender institution is available for male offenders aged 14 to 20 and for female offenders aged 15 to 20. The minimum term is 21 days for males aged 14 to 20 and females aged 17 to 20. For 15 and 16 year old girls sentences must be over 4 months. The maximum term is 4 months for 14 year old boys and 12 months for 15 and 16 year olds of both sexes. (If the maximum term for which an adult could be sentenced to imprisonment is less than 4 or 12 months as the case may be, the maximum term of detention in a young offender institution is the same as the maximum term of imprisonment). For 17 to 20 year olds the maximum term is the same as the maximum term of imprisonment for the offence for an adult.

10.6   Male juveniles and those male young adult offenders sentenced to four months or less are committed directly from court to a young offender institution. Offenders in these groups are normally held either in a self-contained wing or in a wholly separate establishment. Other offenders sentenced to detention in a young offender institution are normally held for a short period in an allocation unit before being allocated to an appropriate young offender institution. The allocation is based on an assessment of the offenders' suitability for open, closed or long term conditions and of their need for special psychiatric or medical facilities. Some male offenders in this group who have a relatively short time to serve, due to time spent in custody on remand, may be allocated to an establishment or wing specialising in provision for shorter sentenced inmates. Young offenders sentenced to detention in a young offender institution may only be held in prison in certain circumstances such as for allocation for medical purposes or other reasons as directed by the Secretary of State. Offenders under 17 may only be held in a prison for a temporary purpose.

10.7   The Young Offender Institution Rules define the aim of a young offender institution as "to help offenders to prepare for their return to the outside community". They aim to provide inmates with flexible but coherent programmes consisting of regime activities such as work, education, physical education and other training and community service. Preparation of inmates for release is carried out in co-operation with the services responsible for their subsequent supervision. At institutions holding juveniles and short-sentenced young adults the relatively short time spent by inmates before release dictates the need for a brisker approach. There is an emphasis on getting inmates involved in the routine of the establishment as quickly as possible. Education and training are organised in short modules so that, however short the sentences, inmates have the opportunity of completing courses and obtaining certificates of achievement. Juveniles of compulsory school age must receive a minimum of 15 hours education a week. At institutions for inmates serving longer terms it is possible to provide a more extensive programme; vocational training and work form an important part of the regime for older inmates and those serving longer sentences.

10.8   The period served under a sentence of detention in a young offender institution may be reduced in the same way as the period served under a sentence of imprisonment, by remission of one-third of the sentence for those sentenced to over 12 months and by one-half for those sentenced to 12 months or less. The sentence may also be reduced by any time spent on remand in custody or local authority secure accommodation before the sentence was passed. If the sentence is more than 12 months, the offender becomes eligible for release on licence under the parole scheme after serving six months from the date of sentence or one-third of the sentence whichever is the longer; and if he is released he will be on licence until the end of the second third of the sentence.

10.9   Whether or not he is released on parole, an offender sentenced to detention in a young offender institution is normally subject to statutory supervision on release from custody. The length of the period of supervision depends on the length of the sentence and the age of the offender. It is not normally less than 3 months and usually lasts from the date of the offender's release until the end of the full period of the sentence. It is never more than 12 months, and never extends beyond the offender's 22nd birthday. On release, the offender will be issued with a notice of supervision which sets out the requirements specified by the Secretary of State. Failure to comply with the requirements of this supervision is punishable by a fine or a custodial sentence of not more than 30 days. Statutory supervision does not, however, unlike a parole licence, carry a liability for the offender to be recalled to complete serving the original sentence. In some cases, an offender may be released on licence before he has served the second third of the sentence, and then be subject to statutory supervision until the end of the sentence. For instance, an offender sentenced to 18 months may be paroled after 6 months, he will be subject to a parole licence for the next 6 months and then subject to statutory supervision until the end of the original 18 months (unless he reaches 22 before this time). The period of parole and subsequent supervision should not in aggregate exceed 12 months.

Detention in a Place Approved by the Secretary of State

10.10   The maximum period of detention in a young offender institution to which an offender under 17 may be sentenced is 12 months. If he has committed a very serious offence, however, the court may consider it necessary for him to be detained for a longer period. A juvenile who has been found guilty by the Crown Court of an offence, other than murder which, in the case of an adult, would be punishable with imprisonment for 14 years or more, may be ordered to be detained under Section 53(2) of the Children and Young Persons Act 1933. Only the Crown Court may order this form of detention, and it may do so only when the juvenile has been committed for trial and convicted on indictment. Detention under section 53(2) is not available where there is a summary trial followed by committal for sentence. This means that if a juvenile is charged with an offence of the kind mentioned above, and if the juvenile court takes the view that the offence is so serious that, were he or she to be convicted, detention under section 53(2) should be among the disposals available, it will be appropriate to commit the juvenile for trial. (The power to commit to the Crown Court in these circumstances is available only in respect of juveniles aged 14 or older. There is an exception for those charged with manslaughter where the lower age limit is 10 years. Those charged with manslaughter *must* be committed to the Crown Court for trial. For murder see paragraph 10.12.) It should be stressed, however, that in reaching this decision, the Juvenile Court should bear in mind that this disposal is intended to be used only for the most serious offences. The fact that a juvenile is charged with an offence for which detention under section 53(2) is available does not itself mean that this disposal will be appropriate in his case if he is found guilty. The law restricts the use of the power to those cases where the court considers that none of the other means of dealing with the offender is suitable. Offenders sentenced to detention under section 53(2) are not eligible for the one third remission which applies to sentences of imprisonment but the Home Secretary has power to release them on licence at any time on the recommendation of the Parole Board and to include conditions on the licence. The progress of detainees is kept under review from the time of sentence; if granted parole the offender is subject to the terms of his licence until the expiry of the full period of his sentence.

Detention During Her Majesty's Pleasure
10.11   Juveniles charged with murder must be committed to the Crown Court for trial. Under section 53(1) of the Children and Young Persons Act 1933 anyone found guilty of murder committed when under the age of 18 must be sentenced to detention during Her Majesty's pleasure. Detainees may be released on licence, subject to conditions, on the recommendation of the Parole Board. As with persons sentenced to life imprisonment, the date of release depends on the individual circumstances of the case, and the Lord Chief Justice and the trial judge (if available) must be consulted before release is authorised.

Custody For Life
10.12   Under Section 8 of the Criminal Justice Act 1982 an offender aged 18, 19 or 20 who is found guilty of murder must be sentenced to custody for life. This is also the maximum penalty when an offender aged 17 but under 21 is convicted of any other offence for which an adult would be liable to life imprisonment. The provisions in sections 1 and 2 of the Criminal Justice Act 1982 about the use of custodial sentences for young offenders apply to the sentence (see paragraphs 10.2 and 10.3). An offender who is sentenced to custody for life will be treated for all practical purposes as if he had been sentenced to imprisonment for life. He will normally serve the sentence in a prison and will be released when the Home Secretary decides, on the recommendation of the Parole Board and after consulting the Lord Chief Justice and the trial judge (if available).

Detention in Default or for Contempt
10.13   Occasionally a court will need the power to pass a very short period

of detention on a young offender, either because he has failed to comply with an order of the court to pay a fine or to make some other payment, or because he is in contempt of court – either by disobeying an order of the court, by failing to attend after being released on bail, or by misbehaviour in court. In all of these cases, the court may commit an adult to prison: a young adult offender may be ordered to be detained under the provisions of section 9 of the Criminal Justice Act 1982. There is no minimum term of detention, and the maximum is the same as the maximum period of imprisonment which would apply in the case of an adult. The court must not use this power to deal with an offender under 21 unless it is of the opinion that no other method of dealing with him is appropriate, but the statutory restrictions in Section 1 of the 1982 Act do not apply. There is no statutory obligation on the court to obtain a social inquiry report, although the court must 'obtain and consider information about the circumstances and take into account any information which is before the court which is relevant to his character and mental condition'. If a magistrates' court makes a detention order of this kind, it must state in open court the reason for its opinion that no other method of dealing with him is appropriate. This form of detention is not available for juveniles.

CHAPTER 11

Sentencing Juvenile Offenders

Introduction

11.1   Young people aged under 17 are commonly known as 'juveniles', although for some purposes the law distinguishes between the categories of 'children' (those aged under 14) and 'young persons' (those aged 14 to 16). The purpose of this chapter is to describe the powers of the courts in relation to juveniles who come before them in criminal proceedings. The principal statutory provisions relating to courts' powers in respect of juvenile offenders are to be found in the Children and Young Persons Acts 1933 and 1969 and the Criminal Justice Acts of 1982 and 1988. The Children Act 1989 contains provisions making important changes to courts' powers to sentence juveniles. At the time this book went to press the provisions were not yet in force. They are described in paragraph 11.30.

General principles

11.2   Parliament has enacted a general principle which applies to all courts when dealing with juveniles. It is laid down by the Children and Young Persons Act 1933 section 44(1). This section provides that every court dealing with a child or young person who is brought before it, whether as an offender or otherwise, 'shall have regard to the welfare of the child or young person and shall in a proper case take steps for removing him from undesirable surroundings and for seeing that proper provision is made for his education and training'. This section does not mean that the court may not also consider other matters, such as general deterrence. However, the Court of Appeal has said that a deterrent sentence should not be passed on a juvenile unless the court has 'weighed most carefully in the balance deterrence on the one side against individual treatment for the rehabilitation of the young offender on the other'.

Juvenile Courts

11.3   Most proceedings in respect of juveniles are brought in specially constituted magistrates' courts known as juvenile courts. (For the exceptions see paragraph 11.5.) The procedure in juvenile courts is simpler and less formal than in adult magistrates' courts. Members of the public are not admitted to sittings of juvenile courts but the press may attend and report the proceedings. However, their reports, may not identify any juveniles involved unless the court allows identification so as to prevent injustice to a juvenile. The magistrates who sit in juvenile courts are chosen from a special panel. The court must be made up of not more than three magistrates, among whom there must normally be at least one man and at least one woman.

Criminal proceedings

11.4 The earliest age at which a juvenile can be brought to court in criminal proceedings is 10 years (section 50 of the 1933 Act as amended by section 16 of the Children and Young Persons Act 1963). This is known as the 'age of criminal responsibility'. A juvenile below the age of 10 may not be found guilty of an offence. Between the ages of 10 and 13 a juvenile charged with an offence is presumed not to be able to understand that what he is alleged to have done was wrong. For a juvenile of this age to be found guilty, the prosecution must satisfy the court not only that he committed the offence, but also knew that what he was doing was seriously wrong.

11.5 Juvenile Courts may try a much wider range of offences than adult magistrates' courts. Whatever the offence with which he is charged the juvenile must be tried in a juvenile court unless one of a number of conditions are met. These are:

(a) He is charged with homicide (ie murder or manslaughter). In this case he must be committed to Crown Court for trial.

(b) He is aged 14 or older and charged with an offence for which an adult could be sentenced to at least 14 years imprisonment. If the court considers that, if he is found guilty, it ought to be possible for him to be detained under section 53 of the Children and Young Persons Act 1933 it may commit him to the Crown Court for trial (see paragraph 10.10).

(c) He is charged jointly with a person aged 17 or older, and the court considers that it is in the interests of justice that they should both be committed to the Crown Court for trial.

(d) He is charged jointly with a person aged 17 or older or the proceedings are in another way connected with those of an adult who is to be tried in an adult magistrates' court.

11.6 When a juvenile has been tried in an adult magistrates' court or the

Crown Court, the court may remit him to the juvenile court to decide how he should be dealt with. The court is required by law to do this 'unless satisfied that it would be undesirable to do so.' An adult magistrates' court must remit the juvenile to the juvenile court unless it decides to deal with him by a discharge, or fine, or to bind over his parent or guardian to take proper care and control of him. Advice on the circumstances in which it would be appropriate for the Crown Court to remit a juvenile to the juvenile court for sentence has been given by the Lord Chief Justice. In his view reasons why it might be undesirable for the Crown Court to remit a juvenile to the juvenile court include:

(a) the fact that the judge who presided over the trial might be better informed as to the facts and circumstances;

(b) the risk of disparity if co-defendants were sentenced in different courts on different occasions;

(c) delay, duplication of proceedings and fruitless expense;

(d) the fact that remitting the juvenile might cause difficulty over an appeal, as an appeal against conviction would be to the Court of Appeal whilst an appeal against sentence would be to the Crown Court.

The Lord Chief Justice said that it might be desirable to remit a juvenile where a report had to be obtained and the judge would be unable to sit when the report would be available, but this situation should be avoided when possible by the committing justices giving directions for the preparation of reports before trial.

Disposals available for juvenile offenders
11.7   A summary of the disposals available to the courts in dealing with juvenile offenders is set out in the table below. Some of the powers are the same as those available for dealing with young adults. In some cases there are additional limitations and these are described in paragraphs 11.8 to 11.12. Other powers are available only in respect of juveniles and these are fully described in paragraphs 11.13 to 11.29. The effect of the 1989 Act is described in paragraph 11.30.

For all offences:
Absolute/conditional discharge
Bind Over ⎫
Fine   ⎬ normally payable by parents or guardian
Compensation ⎭
Supervision order, with or without added requirements

For imprisonable offences:
Attendance centre order
Community service order (16 year olds only)

For serious imprisonable offences where there is a need for care or control:
*Care order

For serious imprisonable offences committed by young offenders already subject to a care order:
*Charge and control condition

For imprisonable offences where no alternative is appropriate:
Detention in a young offender institution (for boys from the age of 14 and girls from the age of 15)

For imprisonable offences committed by mentally disordered offenders:
Hospital or guardianship orders

For grave offences tried on indictment only:
Detention in a place approved by the Secretary of State.

*To be abolished by the Children Act 1989.

Fines etc
11.8   Fines, compensation orders and orders to pay the costs of the prosecution may be made against juveniles in much the same way as against adults, but there are some minor points of difference. The maximum fines for juveniles found guilty by a magistrates' court (whether this is an adult magistrates' court or a juvenile court) are £400 for young persons and £100 for children, unless the maximum provided for the offence in the case of an adult is less; if it is, that maximum applies. There is no statutory limit on the amount which the Crown Court may fine a

juvenile who is found guilty on indictment, but the limits mentioned in the previous sentence apply where the Crown Court is dealing with appeals from a magistrates' court or with committals under the Magistrates' Courts Act 1980 section 37. As most juveniles will not have the money to pay a fine or compensation, the law provides that, if a court deals with a juvenile by means of a fine, a compensation order or an order to pay prosecution costs, it must order the money to be paid by the parent or guardian of the juvenile, instead of by the juvenile (section 55 of the 1933 Act as substituted by section 26 of the 1982 Act). This requirement does not apply where the parent or guardian cannot be found or where it would be unreasonable to make an order for payment by the parent or guardian having regard to the circumstances of the case. Where a juvenile is found guilty of an offence, the court may, if the parent or guardian consents, bind the parent or guardian over (technically, called 'ordering him to enter into a recognisance') to take proper care of him and exercise proper control over him. The maximum amount of such a recognisance is £1000.

11.9   A juvenile may not be committed to prison or detention if he fails to pay a fine or a compensation order, although he may be ordered to attend an attendance centre. The court has power to bind over the juvenile's parents to ensure that the juvenile pays the outstanding sum, or it may order the parent to pay the sum himself. In the latter case, the sum may be recovered from the parent as if he had been convicted and the original order had been made against him (section 81 of the Magistrates' Courts Act 1980).

Community service orders
11.10   A juvenile aged 16 may be ordered to perform community service. Community service orders may not be made for juveniles below this age. The requirements of the law are the same as those that apply to offenders aged seventeen or older, with two differences. First, the maximum number of hours service which a 16 year old may be ordered to perform is 120 (as compared to the adult maximum of 240). The second difference is that the court must have been notified that community service arrangements for persons of this age are available in the area where the 16 year old lives. This will normally be the case.

11.11   If the 16 year old fails to carry out the work he is ordered to do, he may be brought back to the court and dealt with in any manner in which he could have been dealt with by the court which made the community service order. This means that, even though he may be aged 17 by the time he is brought before the court for failing to carry out the work, he must be dealt with as if he were still a juvenile. If, in these circumstances, the court decides that a custodial sentence is appropriate, it is bound to obey the restrictions on the use of custody in the case of juveniles.

Attendance Centre Orders
11.12   Attendance Centre Orders are dealt with in *Chapter 8*. There are separate centres for juveniles. The maximum number of hours for which a juvenile may be ordered to attend is 24 (compared with 36 for 17 to 20 year olds). For those under 14, the Court has discretion to order less than the normal minimum of 12 hours.

Disposals available only for juveniles

Care Orders
11.13   Any court dealing with a juvenile found guilty of an offence punishable in the case of an adult with imprisonment may make a care order. The effect of a care order is to transfer to the appropriate local authority all the rights of the parents of the juvenile concerned. It is for the local authority acting through its social services department, to decide how the care order is to be implemented. The juvenile will normally be dealt with in one of three ways. He may be:

(a) allowed to remain at home in the charge and control of his parents, but subject to the right of the local authority to remove him; or
(b) boarded with foster parents; or
(c) required to reside in a community home or voluntary home.

The court has no control over the local authority in deciding between these alternatives (except where it has power to make a charge and control condition – see paragraphs 11.18 – 11.21).

11.14   A number of conditions must be fulfilled before a court may make a care order in criminal cases. The court must be of the opinion both that a care order is appropriate because of the seriousness of the offence, and that the juvenile is in need of care or control which he is unlikely to receive unless the court makes a care order. These conditions are not alternatives: they must both be satisfied. A further condition is that the court may not make a care order in respect of a juvenile who is not legally represented in the court. There are certain exceptions to this last condition.

11.15   A care order normally lasts until the juvenile reaches the age of 18. However, if he is already 16 when the care order is made, it lasts until he is 19. Either the juvenile or the local authority may apply to the juvenile court to bring the care order to an end before this time. If the court decides to bring the order to an end, it may replace the care order with a supervision order for a period not exceeding three years or until the person attains the age of 18 if this is earlier. If a care order is about to come to an end because the person in care will be 18, the local authority may apply to the court for an extension of the order until he is 19. This may be done only if he is accommodated in a community home or similar establishment, and it seems to be both in his interests and in the interests of the public that he should continue to be accommodated there, because of his mental condition or behaviour.

11.16   Sometimes the local authority may decide that it is necessary to restrict the liberty of a juvenile in their care and place him in secure accommodation. Special conditions apply in these cases. In the first instance the use of secure accommodation is a matter for the local authority rather than the court, but if the local authority wishes to keep the juvenile in secure accommodation for more than 72 hours it must apply to the juvenile court for permission. The court does not have authority to order, on its own initiative, that a juvenile subject to a care order should be detained in secure accommodation. This restriction applies whether the court is making an initial care order or adding a charge and control condition to an existing care order.

11.17   The court's power to make care orders in criminal proceedings is to be abolished by the 1989 Act (see paragraph 11.30).

The charge and control condition
11.18   In certain circumstances a court may add what is known as a 'charge and control condition' to an existing care order. The court may do this when a juvenile who is already subject to a care order made either in criminal proceedings or in care proceedings based on the offence condition (ie where the ground for making the care order is the commission of an offence) is found guilty of a further offence. The further offence need not have been committed whilst the care order was in force. The effect of the charge and control condition is to prevent the local authority in whose care the juvenile has been placed by the care order from allowing him to remain in the charge and control of his parents or other specified persons. The local authority must either board him with foster parents or require him to live for the time being in a community home or a voluntary home. A court may make a charge and control condition only if it is of the opinion both that it is appropriate to do so because of the seriousness of the offence, that no other method of dealing with the offender is appropriate.

11.19 A charge and control condition may include an exception allowing the local authority to permit the juvenile to remain in the charge and control of a specified person, including a parent. For instance, in the case of a juvenile whose parents are separated, the court might impose a charge and control condition with an exception allowing the local authority to permit the child to live with one parent but not the other. The charge and control condition lasts for a period of not more than six months which the court specifies. A further condition may be made if before the specified period has expired the juvenile is found guilty of a further imprisonable offence.

11.20 The juvenile in whose case a charge and control order is made may appeal, either to the Crown Court or to the Court of Appeal as appropriate. If the condition is made by a juvenile court, the local authority may appeal to the Crown Court against the condition. The parents have no right of appeal as such. A condition may be revoked or varied by a juvenile court.

11.21 The court's power to impose a charge and control condition is to be abolished by the 1989 Act (see paragraph 11.30).

Supervision orders
11.22 A supervision order (made under section 7(7) of the 1969 Act) is in some ways the equivalent for juveniles of a probation order, but there are a number of differences. The most important is that it is not necessary to have the consent of the juvenile to the making of the order, although his consent is necessary if certain requirements are to be included. A supervision order may be made when a juvenile is found guilty of any offence. It places the juvenile under the supervision of a supervisor for the period specified in the order. There is no specified minimum period. The maximum period is three years. The supervisor will be either the local authority (in the person of a local authority social worker) or a probation officer. A probation officer may be appointed as supervisor of a child under 13 only on the request of the local authority and if a probation officer is already supervising a member of the child's household.

11.23 A supervision order may include a variety of different kinds of requirements relating to things which the juveniles must do or not do during the period of the order. The statutory provisions are set out in sections 12 to 12C of the 1969 Act. The provisions have been heavily amended. In their consolidated form they are to be found in schedule 10 to the 1988 Act. The details of the law are complicated, but the general effect is to give the court which makes a supervision order the choice between deciding for itself what detailed requirements to make and then including them in the order, or delegating authority to the supervisor to give detailed directions to the juvenile.

11.24 Authority to give directions may be delegated to the supervisor (under section 12(2) of the 1969 Act) only if there is in force locally a scheme of what is known as intermediate treatment. Intermediate treatment consists of a wide variety of recreational, educational or socially valuable activities designed to secure the involvement of the juvenile within a community context. Some intermediate treatment facilities provide highly intensive forms of community-based supervision. The term itself indicates the the provision is 'intermediate' between the removal of the juvenile from home and relying solely on the support of social work with the juvenile or his family. Intermediate treatment schemes, which are drawn up by the local authority social services department in consultation with the local probation service consist of lists of intermediate treatment facilities that are available locally. All local authority areas are required to have a scheme.

11.25 If the court delegates authority to give directions, the supervisor, at his own discretion, may require the juvenile to do any or all of the following things.

(a) live at a particular place for a specified period

(b) attend at a specified place at specified times

(c) take part in various forms of activity (eg at an intermediate treatment facility listed in a scheme).

More than one type of requirement may be attached at a time.

The court does not specify any of the details of the requirements in the supervision order, as they are the responsibility of the supervisor. However, the court does set the number of days on which the supervisor may require the juvenile to comply with his directions. The maximum number of days is 90, but these need not be consecutive.

11.26 Where the court does not delegate authority to the supervisor but itself decides what requirements to attach to the supervision order, it may choose from among a number of types of requirement (section 12A of the 1969 Act).

(a) *Positive requirements*. Here, the court may itself impose any of the sorts of requirements that are described at (a), (b) and (c) in the previous paragraph.

(b) *Night restriction*. This requires the juvenile to remain at a specified place or places (one of which must be his home) for specified periods between 6 pm and 6 am (but not more than 10 hours on any one night), unless he is accompanied by his parent, guardian, the supervisor or by some person specified in the order. It is limited to a period of not more than 30 days in all (not necessarily consecutive) during the first three months of the supervision order.

(c) *Negative requirements*. These are instructions to the juvenile that he must not take part in specified activities, either on a specified day or days during the currency of the supervision order, or during the whole or a specified part of the supervision order. The 90 day limit does not apply.

More than one type of requirement may be attached at the same time.

11.27 Before including in a supervision order any of the requirements described in the previous paragraph the court must do a number of things. It must:

(a) consult the supervisor about the juvenile's circumstances and the feasibility of securing the juvenile's compliance with the requirement; and

(b) be satisfied that the requirement is necessary to secure the good conduct of the juvenile or to prevent him committing more offences; and

(c) obtain the consent of the juvenile (or his parent or guardian in the case of a child under 14), and of any other person whose co-operation would be involved in carrying out the requirement.

11.28 There are two other types of requirement that the court may attach to supervision orders.

(a) *Requirement for mental treatment* (section 12B of the 1969 Act). Where the court is satisfied on medical evidence that the mental condition of the supervised person requires and is susceptible to treatment, it may require him to receive treatment. Where the juvenile is aged 14 or over his consent is required. This requirement may be attached in addition to or in place of any of the requirements described in paragraph 11.26.

(b) *School attendance requirement* (section 12C of the 1969 Act). The court has the power to require a supervised juvenile of compulsory school age to attend school or comply with other arrangements that may have been made for his education. The juvenile's consent is not required, but the court must consult the local education authority about the arrangements for his education before imposing the requirement. It must also consult the supervisor and must be satisfied that the requirement is necessary to secure the good conduct of the juvenile or to prevent his offending further. This requirement is not available where the supervised juvenile is required to comply with directions given by the supervisor.

11.29   The provisions of the law governing the court's powers to deal with a juvenile who does not observe the requirements of a supervision order made in respect of him are complicated. (They are set out in section 15 of the 1969 Act, which was amended by the 1988 Act, Schedule 10.) The basic position is that, for breach of any requirement (*except* the requirement for mental treatment) the court has power to fine the juvenile up to £100 or make an attendance centre order in respect of him. The law provides stronger sanctions where the court has certified (under section 12D of the 1969 Act) that the supervision order was made instead of a custodial sentence. In such cases, the court may discharge the supervision order and deal with the juvenile as if it had just convicted him of the original offence. These stronger sanctions are available *only* where the supervision order contains one or more the requirements of the kind described in paragraph 11.26. Slightly different provisions apply in the case of supervised offenders aged 17 or 18.

The Children Act 1989
11.30   When the relevant provisions come into force, the 1989 Act will make some important changes to the sentencing arrangements for juvenile offenders. The court's powers to make a care order in criminal proceedings, and to impose a charge and control condition will be abolished. There will be a new power for the court to include a "residential requirement" in supervision orders. This will require the supervised juvenile to live in accommodation provided by or on behalf of the local authority. The court will have the power to specify named people with whom the juvenile must not live. This requirement will be able to be attached to a supervision order where:

(a) the juvenile has been convicted of an imprisonable offence; and

(b) the court is satisfied that the offending behaviour is due, to a significant extent to the circumstances in which the juvenile has been living; and

(c) when the juvenile committed the offence, he was subject to a care order which had been made in criminal proceedings or to a supervision order including a "residence requirement" or to which had been attached requirements of the kind described in paragraph 11.26 and

(d) the court is of the opinion that the offence is serious.

The maximum duration of the requirement will be six months. Before imposing it the court must consult the local authority and must have obtained and considered a social inquiry report. When the relevant provisions of the 1989 Act come into force extant care orders made in criminal proceedings will lapse after 6 months unless they have expired or been discharged earlier.

CHAPTER 12

Mentally Disordered Offenders

Mentally disordered offenders
12.1 Considerations other than deterrence and retribution are particularly relevant when determining cases of mentally disturbed offenders. Above all the basic principle applicable in all cases, that custody must be used only as a last resort, applies with particular force in respect of the mentally disturbed. It will seldom be appropriate – or effective – to give a mentally disturbed offender a custodial sentence. In particular, such action should not be be regarded as a means of securing for the offender such psychiatric treatment as he needs.

12.2 Most of the special powers described below apply where the person before the court is considered to be suffering from "mental disorder" within the meaning of the Mental Health Act 1983. There are, however, many others whose condition does not fall within the scope of the 1983 Act who are nevertheless suffering from some form of mental disturbance or disorder. When the use of powers under the Mental Health Act 1983 is not appropriate, it will nevertheless be right to take account of the defendant's mental condition in deciding what disposal is appropriate. The courts have available to them a wide range of non-custodial options. For a comparatively minor offence by a mentally disturbed offender, absolute or conditional discharge may well be sufficient sanction. For more serious offences a probation order might be a suitable means of providing a mentally disturbed offender with help in coping with the problems and difficulties which have led to his offending. In particular, when the offender does not need to be detained in hospital, but is suffering from a mental condition which needs treatment and can be treated, the courts have power to make a probation order including a requirement that the probationer submits to psychiatric treatment – described more fully in paragraph 12.10.

12.3 The law gives the courts a variety of powers to deal with offenders who are not so mentally disordered as to be absolved from criminal responsibility for their actions but are nevertheless suffering from one of the 4 categories of mental disorder defined in the Mental Health Act 1983 and in need of psychiatric treatment. Some of those powers may be exercised without proceeding to conviction: the Crown Court may in certain circumstances remand to hospital for treatment accused persons who are waiting to be tried as well as those waiting to be sentenced. Magistrates' courts have power to make a hospital order without convicting the defendant, but they must first be satisfied that the defendant did the act or made the omission with which he is charged. Those who have been found guilty may be sent to hospital under an interim hospital order or a hospital order and in some cases a hospital order may be made in conjunction with a restriction order. Alternatively, they may be put on probation with a requirement that they undergo psychiatric treatment, or be made subject to a guardianship order.

12.4   The psychiatric facilities which the courts may use for these purposes ar the same as those provided by the National Health Service for the treatment of non-offender patients. With the exception of the four 'special hospitals' (Broadmoor, Rampton, Moss Side and Park Lane) which provide treatment in conditions of highest security any given psychiatric hospital will as a general rule admit patients only from a particular catchment area, from which each prospective patient must come or with which he must have some connection. Furthermore, different hospitals specialise in the treatment of different forms of mental disorder, so that in any one catchment area there are likely to be at least two psychiatric hospitals, one providing treatment for mental illness and one for mental handicap. For this reason the legislation provides that the consent of the receiving hospital is required before the courts may order an offender's admission. Where the court has it in mind to make a hospital order or an interim hospital order, Regional Health Authorities are now required to assist the courts in identifying an appropriate hospital for any particular offender (see para. 12.17).

Obtaining psychiatric reports
12.5   It is clearly *desirable* that when the court suspects that a defendant may be mentally disturbed it should ensure that it has before it evidence as to the defendant's mental condition. Before the court may exercise any of its powers under the Mental Health Act 1983 it *must* first obtain and consider such evidence. Often such evidence will already have been commissioned by the defence. In other cases it may be necessary to adjourn the case (usually for a minimum of 7 days) so that such evidence can be obtained (see Adjournment and Deferment, paragraph 3.23), or to remand the defendant on bail or in custody. A mentally disturbed defendant has the same right to a presumption in favour of bail as any other defendant. Before deciding that it is necessary to remand a defendant

in custody in order to secure the preparation of medical reports; the possibility should be considered of making it a condition of bail that the defendant should attend or reside at a psychiatric hospital to help the preparation of reports. The courts have power to remand an accused person to a hospital for a report on his mental condition. The Crown Court may remand to hospital for report anyone who is waiting for his trial before the Crown Court for an offence punishable with imprisonment, or who has been brought before the court for such an offence but has not as yet been dealt with. A magistrates' court may remand to hospital anyone who has been found guilty of an offence punishable with imprisonment and anyone who is charged with such an offence (but not yet convicted) if either the person consents to the remand to hospital or the court is satisfied that he did the act or made the omission with which he is charged (although he may not technically be guilty, because of his mental state). Before remanding an accused person to hospital for a report, the court must be satisfied on the evidence (which may be written or oral) of a medical practitioner approved under the Mental Health Act 1983 as having special experience in the diagnosis or treatment of mental disorder, that there is reason to suspect that the accused person is suffering from mental illness, psychopathic disorder, severe mental impairment or mental impairment; in addition, the court must think that it would be impracticable for a report to be made on the accused person's mental condition if he were remanded on bail. Before remanding an accused person to hospital for a report the court must also be satisfied, on the evidence either of the medical practitioner who is to make the report or of a person representing the managers of the hospital to which the accused is to be admitted (which must be specified), that arrangements have been made for the accused to be admitted to the hospital within seven days of the remand. The court may give directions for his custody in a place of safety pending admission.

12.6 The period for which an accused person may be remanded to hospital for a report must not be more than 28 days in the first instance. The court may remand him for further periods of not more than 28 days at a time, if it is satisfied on the evidence of the medical practitioner who is to make the report that a further period of remand is necessary to allow the assessment of his mental condition to be completed. The accused person must not be remanded in this way for a total period of more than twelve weeks. (The accused person does not need to be brought to the court for the purpose of a further remand, so long as he is represented by counsel or solicitor and his representative is given the opportunity to be heard.)

12.7 The court may end the remand at any time. The accused person is entitled to obtain (at his own expense) an independent report on his mental condition from a medical practitioner chosen *by himself.* If he does so, he may apply to the court for the remand to be ended on the basis of the report.

Remands to hospital for treatment
12.8   Only the Crown Court may remand an accused person to hospital for treatment. The Crown Court may remand anyone who is in custody waiting to be tried by the Crown Court, or anyone who at any time before sentence is in custody in the course of a trial before the court. The accused person must be charged with an offence punishable with imprisonment, but the power to remand to hospital for treatment may not be used during proceedings against a person charged with murder, although it may be used in the case of a person who has been found guilty of manslaughter by reason of diminished responsibility or otherwise on an indictment for murder, if the court adjourns between conviction and sentence. Any person who has been committed by the Crown Court, on bail, or who is on bail after being convicted by the Crown Court, may not be remanded to hospital for treatment.

12.9   More medical evidence is required for a remand for treatment than for a remand for reports. The court must receive the evidence of two medical witnesses, one of whom is approved as having special experience in the diagnosis or treatment of mental disorder, and the court must be satisfied that the accused is suffering from mental illness or severe mental impairment; accused persons suffering from psychopathic disorder or mental impairment (as distinct from severe mental impairment) may not be remanded for treatment, although they may be remanded for reports. Apart from this, the requirements as to procedure and time limits (maximum of 28 days at a time, total period of twelve weeks) and the right of the accused to apply for termination of a remand, are the same as in the case of a remand for reports.

Psychiatric probation orders
12.10   A probation order including a requirement that the probationer submits to psychiatric treatment is often described for convenience as a 'psychiatric probation order'. It is a normal probation order which has been adapted to meet the needs of an offender who does not need to be detained in a hospital, but who is suffering from a mental condition which can be treated and needs treatment. The court makes a probation order in the normal way, with the consent of the offender; but if it is satisfied on the evidence of a medical practitioner approved as having special experience in the diagnosis or treatment of mental disorder that the offender needs treatment for his mental condition but does not need to be detained in

hospital, the court may include in the probation order a requirement that he undergoes medical treatment with a view to the improvement of his mental condition. The court must specify that the offender should be treated either as a voluntary in-patient at a hospital or nursing home (but not at a special hospital), provided that the hospital can arrange admission for him, or as an out-patient at a clinic or other place, or that he should be given treatment under a doctor named in the order. The precise form of the treatment is not specified by the court. The doctor responsible for the offender's treatment may arrange for the offender to be treated at a hospital or clinic which is not mentioned in the order, if the offender agrees. If he does, this treatment is regard as treatment required by the probation order. The offender may be required to undertake treatment for the whole of the period of the probation order, or for part of it. If he fails to undergo the treatment which the probation order requires, the offender is in breach of probation and may be dealt with in the same way as any other offender who is in breach of probation. (It is not considered to be a breach of the probation order if the offender refuses to take surgical, electrical or other irreversible treatment, and the court thinks it was reasonable for him to refuse in all the circumstances.)

Guardianship orders
12.11   An alternative to a psychiatric probation order in some cases may be a guardianship order, which places the offender under the guardianship of either the local authority social services department or of some person approved by the local authority (such as a relative). The conditions for the making of a guardianship order are essentially the same as those for a hospital order (see below).

12.12   The effect of a guardianship order is to give the guardian power to require the patient to live at a specified place, to attend special places at specified times for medical treatment, occupation, education or training and to allow access to any doctor, approved social worker or other person specified by the guardianship. In this way guardianship enables a relative or social worker to help a mentally disordered person to manage in his own home or a hostel, where the alternative would be admission to a hospital. There is however no sanction available to the court in the event of non-compliance with a guardianship order as there is with a psychiatric probation order.

Interim hospital orders
12.13   An interim hospital order may be made by the Crown Court or by a magistrates' court. The offender must be convicted of an offence

86

punishable with imprisonment (except murder), and the court must be satisfied, on the written or oral evidence of two medical practitioners, one of whom is approved as having special experience in the diagnosis or treatment of mental disorder, that the offender is suffering from mental illness, psychopathic disorder, severe mental impairment or mental impairment. The court must also be satisfied that there is reason to suppose that the mental disorder from which the defendant is suffering is such that it may be appropriate for a hospital order to be made. Before making the interim hospital order, the court must be satisfied that arrangements have been made for the admission of the offender to a particular hospital within 28 days of the making of the order. (One of the medical practitioners whose evidence is being taken into account must be employed at the specified hospital). An interim hospital order lasts for a period specified by the court in the first instance, which must not be more than twelve weeks. The order may be renewed for further periods of 28 days at a time, up to a maximum of six months. (It is not necessary for the offender to appear for the order to be renewed, as long as he is represented and his representatives are afforded a hearing by the court.)

12.14   At the end of the period of the interim order the offender's case is considered by the court again. The court may either substitute a hospital order or deal with the offender in some other way. The offender does not need to appear at the end of the interim hospital order if the court intends to make a hospital order but he must be represented at the hearing when this is done: he must be present if the court intends to make a hospital order with restrictions. If the court decides not to make a hospital order, it is free to impose any other form of sentence which would have been available when the offender was originally convicted. (An offender who absconds from the hospital may be arrested and brought back before the court, where he may be dealt with in any way in which the court could have dealt with him for the offence if no interim hospital order had been made.)

Hospital orders
12.15   A hospital order may be made by either the Crown Court or a magistrates' court. It allows the offender to be taken to a hospital and detained there until he is discharged either by the hospital authorities or by the Mental Health Review Tribunal. Anyone convicted of an offence punishable by imprisonment (except murder) can be dealt with by means of a hospital order, provided that the court is satisfied that certain conditions are met. (A magistrates' court may also make a hospital order in the case of a person suffering from mental illness or severe mental impairment without convicting the offender, it it is satisfied that he did the

act or made the omission with which he is charged.) These conditions are:

(a) that the court is satisfied, on the written or oral evidence of two medical practitioners, one of whom is approved as having special experience in the diagnosis or treatment of mental disorder, that the offender is suffering from mental illness, psychopathic disorder, severe mental impairment or mental impairment;

(b) that the mental disorder from which he is suffering is of a nature or degree which makes it appropriate for him to be detained in a hospital for medical treatment;

(c) in the case of an offender suffering from psychopathic disorder or mental impairment, that treatment is likely to alleviate or prevent a deterioration of his condition;

(d) that the court considers, having regard to all the circumstances, including the nature of the offence and the character and antecedents of the offender, and to the other methods of dealing with them, that a hospital order is the most suitable method of dealing with the case; and

(e) that the court is satisfied on the evidence of the doctor who would be responsible for his treatment, or on the evidence of the managers of the hospital, that arrangements have been made for him to be admitted to the hospital within 28 days of the order being made.

12.16 If the court makes a hospital order it must not sentence the offender to any custodial sentence, impose a fine, or make a probation order for the offence. If the offender is a juvenile, the court may make a care order, but it may not make a supervision order or require the parent or guardian to be bound over to take proper care of him or exercise proper control. Any other kind of order (such as a compensation order, or an order disqualifying the offender from driving) may be made. The court may give directions for the offender to be detained in a suitable place until he can be admitted to the specified hospital.

12.17 A hospital order cannot be made unless there is a hospital which is willing to accept the offender as a patient: the court has no power to order a hospital to accept any particular person as a patient. Sometimes there is difficulty finding a hospital which is willing or able to accept an offender: to help the court with this problem, the law provides that the court may require the appropriate Regional Health Authority (normally the Authority for the region where the offender resides or last resided) to provide information about hospitals in its region or elsewhere which might be able to admit the offender. (This does not mean that the Authority must find the offender a place.)

12.18   In the case of admission to a special hospital the person concerned must be regarded as requiring treatment under conditions of special security on account of his/her dangerous violent or criminal propensities. The Court of Appeal has emphasised the very serious situation that has to be established to warrant admission.

Restriction orders
12.19   Where a hospital order is made in respect of an offender by the Crown Court, the court may also make a restriction order if it considers that it is necessary to make such an order for the protection of the public from serious harm, having regard to the nature of the offence, the offender's record and the risk of his committing further offences if set at large. A restriction order may not be made unless at least one of the medical practitioners whose evidence is taken into account when a hospital order is made has given oral evidence to the court. The order is either for an indefinite period ("without limit of time") or for a fixed period. The effect of the order is to prevent the offender from being discharged from hospital, granted leave of absence, or transferred to another hospital, without the approval of the Home Secretary. Alternatively, a restricted patient may, under certain circumstances, be discharged by a Mental Health Review Tribunal.

Imprisonment
12.20   The prison medical services seek to do what they can, both directly and through their working contacts with the NHS, including consultant psychiatrists, to help mentally disordered people who, as a last resort, the courts send to prison. At a very small number of prison establishments specialist facilities have been developed, offering a range of therapies in suitable cases. Effort continues to be made to improve the level and quality of care and support which the prison service is able to provide. But in general terms the fact of imprisonment and the overcrowding and conditions in prisons are not conducive to a healing environment.

12.21   For those reasons it would be wrong to proceed on the basis that such facilities as exist in the prison service are comparable to psychiatric hospitals in the community. It would be unsafe to reach judgments on the assumption that an offender is ensured of treatment while serving a prison sentence. And it follows that, as courts have no authority on the question of to which prison a particular offender might be allocated, it would be wrong to indicate to an offender that he or she would receive psychiatric treatment in prison.

CHAPTER 13

Disqualification from Driving

13.1 A court convicting an offender of one of the more serious offences involving motor vehicles may disqualify that person from driving a motor vehicle and from holding or obtaining a driving licence. The disqualification of drivers whose conduct has proved a danger to other road users can to some extent serve a basic public protection purpose. In most cases, however, the main functions of disqualifications are to punish misuse or careless use of vehicles and to deter both the offender and others from indulging in it. Disqualification can thus be seen as part of the basic penalty imposed by the court for the offence, rather than as an independent order. But although disqualification may be – and sometimes must be – imposed for a road traffic offence, it follows from the conviction, not from the imposition of any particular sentence. The law provides no limit on the length of a period of disqualification, but the Court of Appeal has advised against the use of very long periods of disqualification unless the defendant is a menace to other road users. An offender who is disqualified for a very long period is particularly likely to commit further offences of driving while disqualified rather than complying with the order, as he might were the term more realistic. This is particularly so where the offender is young. Another possible ground for mitigating the term of disqualification which the offence would otherwise merit (though not – see paragraph 13.5 – for waiving obligatory minimum periods) is its effect on the offender's employment prospects.

13.2 There are four different situations in which a court may disqualify an offender from driving:

(a) obligatory disqualification for certain particularly serious offences;

(b) discretionary disqualification for certain other road traffic offences;

(c) disqualification by the accumulation of 'penalty points' for a series of offences;

(d) disqualification where the motor vehicle has been used in the course of committing a non-road traffic offence.

The different considerations governing the use of disqualification in these categories are discussed in the following paragraphs.

Obligatory disqualification

13.3   The offences for which disqualification is obligatory are:

(a) manslaughter by the driver of a motor vehicle;

(b) causing death by reckless driving;

(c) reckless driving committed within three years of a similar offence or an offence of causing death by reckless driving;

(d) driving, or attempting to drive, while unfit through drink or drugs;

(e) driving, or attempting to drive, with an excess concentration of alcohol in the breath, blood or urine;

(f) failing without reasonable excuse, when driving or attempting to drive, to supply a specimen of breath, blood or urine;

(g) motor racing or speed trials on the highway.

13.4   Unless there are 'special reasons' for not doing so, the court must disqualify a driver convicted of any of these offences for at least twelve months or 2 years if the offence was causing death by reckless driving. For a driver convicted of a drink/driving offence committed within ten years of a previous conviction for such an offence, the minimum period is three years. If for special reasons the court decides to impose a shorter term than the minimum, or not to disqualify the offender at all, it must state the grounds for that decision in open court.

13.5   The concept of 'special reasons' has been considered in detail by the Court of Appeal and by the Divisional Court. A 'special reason' must be an extenuating factor directly relating to the offence and to the immediate circumstances in which it was committed. 'Special reasons' do not apply where there are particular circumstances relating to the impact of the penalty on the offender or some other person by causing hardship, inconvenience or loss of employment. Nor can it be a special reason in excess alcohol cases that the offender's alcohol level was only just above the statutory limit, that his ability to drive was not affected or that he did not cause any danger to other road users. There may be a special reason if the offender has consumed alcohol when not expecting to have to drive again that day, and was then faced with a sudden emergency requiring him to drive again, but only if the emergency was a compelling one and the offender had no alternative means of dealing with it.

13.6   'Special reasons' are not a defence to the charge, but they are an issue which, if they are raised, must be raised by the defendant. The defendant must call evidence to prove the facts which it is claimed amount to special reasons (unless those facts are not disputed by the prosecution) and the facts must be established – not beyond reasonable doubt, but as more probable than not (ie 'on the balance of probabilities'). The court must then consider whether those facts can amount to special reasons. The prosecution is entitled to address the court on this point. If the court decides that they can, it may go on to consider whether it does in fact think that the circumstances of the case as a whole justify not disqualifying for the minimum period. Establishing facts which can amount to a valid reason for not imposing the normally obligatory penalty does not mean that the court must not impose it – only that it is not obliged to.

Discretionary disqualification
13.7   Discretionary disqualification applies to other specified road traffic offences which, unlike those carrying obligatory disqualification, are not invariably a grave matter, but which may still be serious enough to justify a period of disqualification. On convicting a driver of any of these offences, the court must endorse the offender's licence, in the absence of special reasons. The court may not disqualify the offender in his absence, unless the case has been adjourned for this purpose and the defendant so informed. A wide range of offences fall in this category, including such common ones as:

(a) careless driving;

(b) exceeding speed limits;

(c) failing to comply with traffic directions;

(d) failing to stop after or to report an accident;

(e) driving while disqualified;

(f) driving while uninsured.

The decision whether to disqualify a driver convicted of such an offence, and if so for how long, will have particular regard to the circumstances of the offence; it can also take full account of the circumstances of the offender. There is no minimum period of disqualification where disqualification is discretionary and it may be appropriate to impose comparatively short periods of disqualification in some cases, for instance to achieve a salutory effect on a first-time offender.

Disqualification for repeated offences – the penalty points system

13.8   Under the penalty points system a driver who commits a number of offences within a period of three years must be disqualified because of this repeated offending whether or not the particular offence now before the court would in itself justify disqualification. The system only applies to offences carrying obligatory or discretionary disqualification (as discussed in the preceding paragraphs). If the court disqualifies the defendant for the offence, no penalty points are imposed. Otherwise the licence must be endorsed with the details of the offence and the number of penalty points incurred.

13.9   Disqualification under the penalty points system occurs when the driver has, as a result of offences committed within a three year period, accumulated a total of twelve or more penalty points. For most offences the number of points to be imposed is fixed by law, but for some offences which can vary greatly in gravity the court must decide the appropriate number within specified limits. The highest number applying to a single offence is ten (the penalty, for example, for reckless driving); less serious offences carry as few as two (for example, driving while disqualified or under age) or three (for example, contravening construction and use regulations). The offences for which the points are variable are careless or inconsiderate driving (for which the range is from three to nine); using, or causing or permitting use of a motor vehicle uninsured or unsecured against third party risks (from six to eight); failure to give particulars or to report an accident (from eight to ten); and failure to stop after an accident (from eight to ten). If the offender is found guilty of a number of offences committed on the same occasion, penalty points are incurred only for the offence to which the highest number applies (or was imposed by the court). If, for instance, the offender is found guilty of committing on the same occasion reckless driving (ten points), driving without a licence (two) and driving without insurance (six to eight), the licence will be endorsed with ten points – and only ten. The offender is liable to disqualification if twelve or more penalty points have been imposed on him for offences committed within a three year period of which at least one is among those the court is currently dealing with. This means that the court may take into account points imposed for an offence committed later than the one(s) with which it is now dealing, but dealt with earlier by the courts.

13.10   If the total of relevant penalty points is twelve or more, the court must order disqualification for a minimum of six months. If, however, the offender has already been disqualified within the three years before the date on which the latest offence was committed (whether under the penalty points system or for particular offences carrying obligatory or discretionary disqualification), the minimum length of the new disqualification is twelve months. If he has previously been disqualified twice duing the three year period, the minimum length is two years.

13.11 A court may disqualify an offender for a term below the minimum required under the penalty points provisions, or decide not to disqualify at all, if it is satisfied that there are 'grounds for mitigating the normal consequences of the conviction' (commonly known as 'mitigating circumstances'). However it may not do so where one of the offences carries obligatory disqualification. In deciding whether there are any mitigating circumstances, the court must disregard: (a) any circumstances which are alleged to make the offence (or any of the other offences leading to the accumulation of penalty points) not a serious one; (b) hardship, other than exceptional hardship and (c) any circumstances which have been relied on previously in a similar situation – ie to mitigate a penalty points disqualification – in the three years preceding the latest conviction. (As to whether they have been relied on previously, it is for the defendant to satisfy the court they they have not.)

13.12 In imposing a disqualification under the penalty points system, the court imposes a single term, but takes account of all the offences in deciding how long it should be. The disqualification is treated as having been imposed for each of the offences. If the court decides to disqualify the offender for the latest offence because of the circumstances of the offence itself, without considering any previous offence no points are in fact endorsed on the offender's licence for the latest offence. Nevertheless, the court is required in determining the period of disqualification to take into account the number of penalty points that would have been imposed if it had not decided to disqualify the defendant for the offences. If the defendant would then have been liable, under the penalty points system, to disqualification for a minimum period (as set out in paragraph 3.10) the court must not disqualify him for a shorter term.

Disqualification of drivers using vehicles in committing non-road traffic offences
13.13 Disqualification of this kind is quite separate from the powers, discussed in the preceding sections of this chapter, relating to the more serious road traffic offences. It is designed as an additional penalty for offenders who use motor vehicles in committing serious indictable offences. Only the Crown Court may disqualify an offender on these grounds, and only when convicting a person of an offence punishable with two years' imprisonment or more. The power applies when a motor vehicle has been used, by the offender or by an accomplice, to facilitate the commission of such an offence (including the removal of stolen property)

or to escape arrest or detection for it. It is not necessary for the offender to have actually driven the vehicle, or even to have travelled in it, in the course of the offence. The Court of Appeal has frequently advised judges that it is unwise to impose a period of disqualification under this power which will persist long after an offender's release from a prison sentence imposed at the same time if the offender is likely to need a driving licence in order to find employment on release. Such a course might prove a handicap to rehabilitation and a stimulus to further crime.

Disqualification until the offender passes a driving test
13.14 A court convincing an offender of a road traffic offence for which disqualification is obligatory or discretionary may order that the offender be disqualified until passing a driving test. Such an order may be made either independently or in conjunction with disqualification for a specified period. This power is intended as a protective, road safety measure rather than as a punishment. Its purpose is not to humiliate an offending driver but to ensure that a driver whose conduct suggests incompetence or whose driving skills may be fading with age is not allowed to drive until his capability has been reassessed. It may also be used, where an offender is disqualified for a long period, to ensure that the offender is re-tested before returning to driving after a long interval.

Removing a disqualification
13.15 Though the court disqualifying an offender should not take account of this possibility in passing sentence, an offender disqualified for a long term may apply to the court for the removal of the order. If the term was less than four years, an application may be made after two years. If the term was between four and ten years, no application may be made until half the term has elapsed. If the term was more than ten years, an application may be made after five years. The court may grant the application by removing the disqualification either immediately or from a date specified. If the application is refused, the offender must wait at least three months before reapplying. In deciding whether to grant the application, the court should consider the offender's character and conduct since disqualification, the nature of the offence and any other circumstances of the case.

CHAPTER 14

Recommendations for Deportation

14.1   Subject to various limitations, described below, a court sentencing a person aged seventeen or more who is not a British Citizen (according to the British Nationality Act 1981) for an offence punishable with imprisonment may recommend to the Home Secretary that the offender be deported from the United Kingdom. This recommendation is additional to any other penalty imposed for this offence, including life imprisonment (even where that is mandatory). The recommendation is considered by the Home Secretary (see paragraph 14.14) and if he decides to act on it he will make the actual deportation order.

Limitations on deportation
14.2   A British citizen, or any other citizen who has the right of abode in the United Kingdom, may not be deported. In addition, exemption from deportation is provided for those citizens of Commonwealth countries ('Commonwealth citizens'), or of the Republic of Ireland who were ordinarily resident here on 1 January 1973 and who have been ordinarily resident here for the 5 years immediately preceding the conviction.

14.3   Citizens of countries who are members of the European Community ('EC citizens') who are in the United Kingdom exercising their right of free movement under the Treaty of Rome – in the course of their employment, or as dependants of someone who is here in the course of employment – may be deported only if the requirements of EC law, as interpreted by the European Court of Justice, are satisfied. The court must consider that the continued presence of the offender in the UK represents 'a genuine and sufficiently serious threat to the requirements of public policy affecting one of the fundamental interests of society'. The Court of Appeal has ruled that where a recommendation is made in such a case, reasons must be given to the Home Secretary and to the offender.

14.4   Persons recommended for deportation can only be deported if another country or territory can accept them, and certain other restrictions may operate in respect of persons to whom the international conventions

96

relating to the status of stateless persons and to the status of refugees apply.

14.5 The Court of Appeal has stated that the courts should not be concerned with the harshness or oppressiveness of the political systems of other countries. It is inappropriate for a court to express a view about the regime in another country, particularly as the court has no knowledge of the matter except common knowledge, which might be wrong. These are matters for the Home Secretary to consider in deciding whether or not to act on the court's recommendation.

14.6 In accordance with a commitment given to the European Commission on Human Rights, action will not be taken, save in exceptional circumstances, on a recommendation for deportation in the case of an overstayer convicted (of any offence) and recommended for deportation who submits a claim for asylum before a deportation order is signed on the basis of the court's recommendation. Deportation action (if appropriate) will instead be pursued through administrative means under section 3(5) of the Immigration Act 1971 in order to provide an avenue of appeal to an adjudicator (under the appellate arrangements for the 1971 Act) who may then take asylum considerations into account.

Procedure

14.7 A recommendation for deportation may not be made until at least 7 clear days after the offender has been served with a written notice setting out the classes of persons who may be deported and explaining that the burden of proof of non-liability to deportation lies with the defence. Such a notice will normally have been served by the police in a relevant case, but if this has not happened, or if insufficient notice has been given, the court may adjourn the case on conviction for the purpose of fulfilling the service of notice requirement.

14.8 It is open to an offender to appeal to a higher court against a recommendation for deportation or the conviction on which the recommendation is based. Once a deportation order has been made an offender may appeal to an adjudicator against deportation to the specified destination, as opposed to another specified country or territory.

14.9 The defendant, or the defendant's legal representative, should be invited to address the court specifically on the question of a possible recommendation for deportation, which should be carefully examined. If a recommendation is made, reasons should be given, particularly (see paragraph 14.3) in the case of EC citizens.

14.10   Offenders recommended for deportation who are neither detained as a result of the sentence nor released on bail must, unless the court otherwise directs, be detained pending the Home Secretary's decision whether to deport. That decision may take some weeks. The Home Secretary must consider all the facts of the case and any representations, and is in any case precluded from making a deportation order until the time allowed for appeal has expired. Courts making a recommendation, but not imposing a long custodial sentence for the offence should therefore carefully consider whether to make directions on this point. Such directions may impose conditions on a release pending the decision – such as that the offender should live in a particular place or should report to the court or to the police or should not take employment. (This last condition may be considered appropriate in cases where a person has been convicted of working without permission). Courts should also bear in mind that detention in custody (as opposed to bail) pending criminal proceedings is not normally appropriate unless there is reason to suppose that the defendant would abscond or commit further offences.

Criteria for making recommendations for deportation
14.11   The Court of Appeal's guidance is that the issue in deciding whether to recommend deportation is whether the continued presence of the offender in the UK would be to the detriment of the country.

14.12   Those who have committed serious offences or who have long records are suitable for recommendations, as are those who are convicted of immigration offences, but a minor offence will not merit a recommendation. An isolated theft from a shop, for instance, would not normally justify a recommendation, although a series of such offences, or a theft carried out by a member of a gang as part of a planned raid, might do so. A recommendation may also be inappropriate even for an offence of a serious nature, if the offence is an isolated incident in the life of an otherwise law-abiding person.

14.13   The courts should think about the effect of a recommendation for deportation on innocent persons, such as the offender's family. If the effect of a recommendation might be to break up a family, the court should think very carefully before making the recommendation.

14.14   In coming to a decision on whether to deport the Home Secretary considers: the nature of the offence; the extent of the offender's criminal record; the length of the offender's stay in the UK and the strength of the offender's connections with it; the offender's age, personal history and domestic circumstances; any compassionate considerations and any representations made by or on behalf of the offender. Deportation of a first-time offender is unlikely unless the offence is serious, a number of other offences are being taken into consideration or the offence is under the Immigration Act 1971.

CHAPTER 15

Restitution, Forfeiture and other Ancillary Orders

15.1 Apart from disqualification from driving and recommendation for deportation, which have been discussed in the preceding chapters, various other ancillary orders are available to a court when passing sentence. These orders do not stand alone, but may be made at the same time as other sentences are passed for the same offence. They may be used by any court including an adult court dealing with a juvenile by means of a discharge or fine or by requiring a recognisance from the parent or guardian. Ancillary orders are normally deemed to form part of the sentence for the purposes of any appeal against sentence to the Crown Court, except where the order in question is one for payment of costs, for the destruction of an animal, or one in pursuance of an enactment under which the court has no discretion as to its making or its terms; some of the more general and significant ancillary orders are outlined in this chapter.

Restitution and compensation

15.2 Where goods have been stolen and a person is convicted of any offence relating to the theft, the court may order the restoration of the goods, or of other goods bought with the proceeds of realisation to the person entitled to recover them. For this purpose 'stolen' and 'theft' have an extended meaning and include blackmail and obtaining by deception. Restitution orders can be made without any application by or on behalf of the person concerned, and may be made in respect of offences taken into consideration. Where no restitution order is made, the court can make an order for the payment of compensation to the owner out of any money so taken in favour of a bona fide purchaser of, or lender on the security of, the goods. In appropriate circumstances, the court may make orders for both restitution and compensation, for example, when a stolen vehicle is recovered but in a damaged condition. When a court is empowered to make a compensation order but does not do so, it is required to give reasons for this decision.

100

15.3   The Police (Property) Act 1897 provides that, where property has come into the possession of the police in connection with any criminal charge or in the execution of a search warrant, a magistrates' court may, on application by the police or by a claimant of the property , make an order for its delivery to the person who appears to the court to be the owner, or if the owner cannot be ascertained, make such other order as it thinks fit. Regulations made by the Home Secretary govern the disposal of unclaimed property.

Deprivation of property used for criminal purposes

15.4   A court which convicts an offender of any offence may order the forfeiture of property where the offence consists of unlawful possession of the property, or where the property has been used for the purpose of committing the offence, or was intended to be used for that purpose. The court must be satisfied that the property has been lawfully seized from the offender, or was in his possession or under his control at the time of his apprehension, or when a summons was issued. The court may make a forfeiture order whether or not it deals with the offender in any other way, and it may make such orders in conjunction with custodial and non-custodial disposals including orders for probation or conditional or absolute discharge. In making a forfeiture order the court must consider the value of the property, and the likely financial and other effects of an order on the offender. Forfeited property is taken into the possession of the police and disposed of under the Police (Property) Act (see preceding paragraph). A person claiming the property under the Act must satisfy the court that he did not realise that it was to be put to unlawful use.

Confiscation

15.5   Under the terms of the Drug Trafficking Offences Act 1986, before the Crown Court sentences an offender who is convicted of a drug trafficking offence it is required to determine whether the convicted person has ever benefited from trafficking. If it considers that he has, it must make a confiscation order for the amount by which he has benefited, or, if the full amount would not be realisable, the maximum amount that would be realisable. Confiscation orders are intended to cover all benefit that the convicted person has received from drug trafficking activities and are not confined to offences that have been brought to trial. The court may also assume that any or all property held by the convicted person, and any or all property that has been held by him for the last six years, represents his proceeds of drug trafficking, except to the extent that the defendant shows otherwise. Realisable property is defined as all property, even that legitimately held, that can be taken to satisfy a confiscation order and includes property held by a third party to whom the defendant has made a gift.

15.6   This type of confiscation order is enforceable by magistrates' courts in the same way as section 6 of the Act applies the normal fine enforcement procedures, with some modifications. There is no power to remit a confiscation order, and no requirement to conduct a means enquiry before the garnishee procedure. The magistrates' court may exercise its powers to commit the convicted person to custody in default of payment, according to the term set by the Crown Court when it made the order.

15.7   The Crown Court and the magistrates' court have power to order confiscation of the proceeds of all indictable offences, excluding those offences covered by paragraph 15.5, and a small number of summary offences listed in Schedule 4 of the Criminal Justice Act 1988 which are liable to yield exceptional profits to the offender. However the provisions differ from those outlined in paragraph 15.5. The court must be satisfied that the offender has benefited from the offence taken with other offences before the court (including any offences taken into consideration) by a total of at least £10,000, and that the amount of the proposed order is realisable. The amount of the order must be at least £10,000, but must not exceed either the total benefit adjudged to have been derived from the offences in respect of which it is made, or the amount that is realisable, whichever is the lesser. A court may only make such a confiscation order if it has received written notice from the prosecutor, to the effect that it appears that the court would be able to make an order meeting the above conditions. The court may take into account, in deciding whether to make an order, information placed before it showing that the victim of the offence intends or has already instituted civil proceedings against the defendant in respect of loss, injury or damage sustained in connection with the offence. If the court proposes to make both a confiscation order and a compensation order against the same offender in the same proceedings, and it appears that the offender would not have the means to satisfy both orders in full, then the court is required to direct the sums realised under the confiscation order shall be applied in payment of the compensation order to the extent of the shortfall. Magistrates have the same powers to enforce these confiscation orders as they have in respect of confiscation orders made under the Drug Trafficking Offences Act 1986.

Exclusion orders
15.8   Where a court which convicts an offender of an offence committed on licensed premises is satisfied that in committing the offence he resorted to violence or offered or threatened to resort to violence, the court may,

subject to certain provisions, make an order, commonly known as an 'exclusion order', prohibiting him from entering those or any other specified premises without the consent of the licensee or someone acting on his lawful behalf.

15.9   Such an exclusion order remains in effect for the period stated in the order, which shall be not less than 3 months and not more than 2 years. Where a court makes an exclusion order the clerk of the court must send a copy of the order to the licensee(s) of the premises to which the order relates.

15.10   The licensee of licensed premises or someone acting for him may expel from those premises any person who has entered, or whom he suspects of entering the premises, in breach of an exclusion order.

15.11   The penalty for entering premises in breach of a licensed premises exclusion order is a fine not exceeding £400 on a summary conviction, or imprisonment for up to one month, or both. At the same time the court may decide terminating the existing order, or varying it by deleting the name of any specified premises, but the order shall not otherwise be affected by a conviction for non-compliance.

15.12   Where a court convicts an offender of an offence connected with football it may make an exclusion order prohibiting him from entering any premises for the purpose of attending any prescribed football match there. The court must be satisfied that making such an order would help to prevent violence or disorder at or in connnection with prescribed football matches.

15.13   A football exclusion order shall remain in effect for the period specified in the order. This shall be not less than 3 months plus the unexpired period of any earlier order, or, if there is more than one such order, the remainder of the most recent.

15.14   The penalty for entering premises in breach of a football exclusion order is also a fine not exceeding £400 on summary conviction, or imprisonment for 1 month, or both.

15.15   Both types of exclusion order may only be made:
 (a) as an addition to a sentence which is imposed in respect of the offence of which the person is convicted; or
 (b) where an offence was committed in England or Wales, in addition to a probation order or an order discharging him absolutely or conditionally.

103

15.16   The Football Spectators Act 1989 enables the courts to impose restriction orders on those convicted of football related offences if the court considers that would help to prevent violence or disorder at or in connection with a designated match outside England or Wales. Persons subject to restriction orders will be required to report to a police station on the occasion of such football matches.

Summary of Sentences Available
(other than mental health orders – see Chapter 12)

Table 1   Powers available to all Courts

Age Group	Non-Custodial	Custodial
10 and under 14	Absolute/conditional discharge Bind over ⎫ Fine ⎬ normally to be paid by parent or guardian. Compensation Order ⎭ Supervision Order (with or without added requirements). Attendance Centre Order (for boys in most areas; girls only in some). Care Order (to which a charge and control condition may be attached following a subsequent offence).	
14 and under 17	Absolute/conditional discharge Bind over ⎫ Fine ⎬ normally to be paid by parent or guardian. Compensation Order ⎭ Supervision Order (with or without added requirements). Attendance Centre Order (for boys in most areas; girls only in some). Care Order (to which a charge and control condition may be attached following a subsequent offence) Community Service Order (for 16 year olds only).	Detention in a young offender institution (for boys from the age of 14 and girls from the age of 15)
17 and under 21	Absolute/conditional discharge Bind over Fine Compensation Order Probation Order (with or without added requirements). Attendance Centre Order (for boys in some areas only) Community Service Order.	Detention in a young offender institution

Age Group	Non-Custodial	Custodial

21 and over	Absolute/conditional discharge
	    Bind over
	    Fine
	    Compensation Order
	Probation Order (with or without added
	    requirements).
	Community Service Order.
		Imprisonment

Table 2 Powers also available to the Crown Court

Age Group	Non-Custodial	Custodial
10 and under 18*		Detention during Her Majesty's Pleasure (for murder)
14 and under 17**		Detention in a place approved by the Secretary of State (for grave crimes only)
17 and under 21***		Custody for life

Footnotes
*   Age when offence was committed
**   From age 10 for manslaughter only
*** From age 18 at time of offence for murder only

106

Sentences passed by the Courts in England and Wales in 1988

Note: The figures in these tables are independently rounded, and thus do not always add up to the overall totals.

A. Use of sentences by all courts

	Offenders sentenced (thousands)			
Type of sentence or order	All offences	Indictable offences	Summary non-motoring offences	Summary motoring offences
Non-custodial				
Absolute discharge	19.0	2.3	6.5	10.2
Conditional discharge	77.6	50.6	23.4	3.5
Probation order	43.6	36.4	4.5	2.7
Supervision order	7.4	6.8	0.5	0.1
Fine	1248.3	151.7	406.0	690.6
Community service order	35.3	30.4	2.8	2.1
Attendance centre order	8.5	7.5	0.9	−(1)
Care order	0.5	0.5	−(1)	−(1)
Otherwise dealt with	12.3	6.0	5.9	0.3
All non-custodial	1452.5	292.2	450.5	709.5
Custodial				
Young Offender Institution	24.1	23.1	0.9	0.2
Imprisonment:				
Fully suspended	30.9	27.3	1.7	1.9
Partly suspended	2.8	2.7	−(1)	−(1)
Unsuspended	45.2	41.4	1.9	2.0
All custodial	103.0	94.5	4.5	4.1
TOTAL	1555.4	386.6	455.1	713.6

(1) Less than 50

B. Sentencing by all courts for indictable offences

						Offenders sentenced (thousands)					
Type of sentence or order	All offences	Violence against the person	Sexual offences	Burglary	Robbery	Theft & handling stolen goods	Fraud & forgery	Criminal damage	Drugs	Motoring offences	Others
Non-custodial											
Absolute or conditional discharge	52.9	7.9	0.6	4.2	0.1	29.1	3.6	2.1	1.6	1.1	2.5
Probation or supervision order	43.2	3.6	1.0	8.4	0.3	21.3	2.9	1.8	1.0	2.1	0.8
Fine	151.7	20.9	2.3	7.0	0.1	68.8	8.2	3.7	11.2	15.7	13.8
Community service order	30.4	3.7	0.1	6.1	0.2	12.3	1.7	0.8	0.5	3.9	1.1
Attendance centre order	7.3	0.9	—(1)	2.1	0.1	3.2	0.1	0.4	—(1)	0.2	0.2
Care order	0.5	—(1)	—(1)	0.1	—(1)	0.2	—(1)	—(1)	—(1)	—(1)	—(1)
Otherwise dealt with	6.0	2.0	0.2	0.4	0.1	1.3	0.3	0.9	—(1)	0.1	0.7
All non-custodial	292.0	39.0	4.2	28.3	0.9	136.2	16.8	9.7	14.3	23.1	19.1
Custodial											
Young Offender Institution	23.1	3.2	0.3	7.9	1.5	6.4	0.3	0.6	0.2	1.2	1.4
Imprisonment:											
Fully suspended	27.3	4.6	0.6	3.3	0.1	9.5	2.7	0.5	1.2	3.6	1.2
Partly suspended	2.7	0.5	0.2	0.4	—(1)	0.8	0.4	—(1)	0.1	0.1	0.2
Unsuspended	41.4	6.0	2.0	8.5	1.6	10.7	2.6	0.9	2.9	3.5	2.6
All custodial	94.5	14.3	3.1	20.1	3.2	27.4	6.0	2.0	4.4	8.4	5.4
TOTAL	386.6	53.6	7.2	48.5	4.4	163.6	22.7	11.8	18.8	31.5	24.6

(1) Less than 50

C. Proportionate use of sentences for indictable offences

Type of sentence or order	Offenders sentenced (percentages)										
	All offences	Violence against the person	Sexual offences	Burglary	Robbery	Theft & handling stolen goods	Fraud & forgery	Criminal damage	Drugs	Motoring offences	Others
Non-custodial											
Absolute or conditional discharge	14	15	8	9	3	18	16	18	9	4	10
Probation or supervision order	11	7	14	17	8	13	13	16	5	7	3
Fine	39	39	32	14	2	42	36	31	60	50	56
Community service order	8	7	1	13	5	8	7	7	3	12	4
Attendance centre order	2	2	1	4	3	2	-(1)	3	-(1)	1	1
Care order	-(1)	-(1)	1	-(1)	1	-(1)	-(1)	1	-	-(1)	-(1)
Otherwise dealt with	2	4	2	1	3	1	1	7	-	-(1)	3
All non-custodial	76	73	58	58	24	83	74	82	76	73	78
Custodial											
Young Offender Institution	6	6	4	16	35	4	1	6	2	3	6
Imprisonment:											
Fully suspended	7	9	8	7	2	6	12	4	7	11	5
Partly suspended	1	1	3	1	1	-(1)	2	1	1	-(1)	1
Unsuspended	11	11	28	18	38	7	12	8	16	11	11
All custodial	24	27	43	41	76	17	26	17	23	27	22
TOTAL	100	100	100	100	100	100	100	100	100	100	100

(1) Less than 1 per cent

Average Cost of Sentences

Sentence	Average cost per offender per week 1988/89
CUSTODY (overall average)	£288
For Male Offenders	
– Dispersal (ie high security/prisons)	£541
– Other closed training prisons – Cat B	£333
Cat C	£225
– Local prisons and remand centres	£268
– Open adult prisons	£199
– Youth Custody Centres – closed	£311
open	£375
For Female Offenders	
– All establishments	£399
	1987/88
COMMUNITY SERVICE ORDER	£15
PROBATION ORDER	£19
SUPERVISION ORDER	£16

The average cost of each attendance centre order was £153 (1988).

Bibliography

The following list includes: the most important statutes specifying sentencing powers; official publications, circulars and statistics; reference works and academic studies. It is, inevitably, highly selective – in each case the aim is to indicate where an expansion of the summary material in the text might most readily be obtained.

Chapter 2: The Criminal Court System
Harris, Brian T (1988)
> *The Criminal Jurisdiction of Magistrates*, 11th edn, Barry Rose
> *Report of the Interdepartmental (Streatfeild) Committee on the Sentencing of Offenders* (1961) (Chairman: Mr Justice Streatfeild) HMSO, Cmnd 1289.
> *Criminal Statistics*, England and Wales, Published annually, Home Office.
> *Judicial Statistics*, England and Wales, Published annually, Home Office.
> Criminal Justice Act 1988.

Chapter 3: Sentences and Sentencing
Ashworth, Andrew (1983) *Sentencing and Penal Policy*, Weidenfeld and Nicholson.
Brody, Stephen (1975) *The Effectiveness of Sentencing*, Home Office Research Study No. 35
Brody, Stephen and Tarling, Roger (1981) *Taking Offenders out of Circulation*. Home Office Research Study No. 64
Cross, Sir Rupert and Ashworth, Andrew (1981) *The English Sentencing System*, Butterworths
Moxon, David (1988) *Sentencing Practice in the Crown Court*. Home Office Research Study No. 103
Shapland, Joanna (1981) *Between Conviction and Sentence*, Routledge.
Tarling, Roger (1980) *Sentencing Practice in Magistrates' Courts*, Home Office Research Study No. 56
Thomas, D A (1979) *Principles of Sentencing*, Heinemann.
Thorpe, Jennifer (1979) *Social Inquiry Reports, A Survey*. Home Office Research Study No. 48

Walker, Nigel (1985) *Sentencing: Theory, Law and Practice*, Butterworths.
Home Office Circular No. 17/1983, *Social Inquiry Reports: General Guidance on Contents.*
Home Office Circular No. 18/1983, *Social Inquiry Reports: Recommendations Relevant to Sentencing.*

Chapter 4: Absolute and Conditional Discharges
Powers of Criminal Courts Act 1973: section 7 (as amended by the Criminal Law Act 1977, S.57); and section 12.

Chapter 5: Financial Penalties
Criminal Justice Act 1982: Part III
Magistrates' Courts Act 1980: Part III (as amended by the Criminal Justice Act 1982 sections 38, 46, 51 and Schs 14 and 16)
Powers of Criminal Courts Act 1973: Sections 35, 36 (as amended by the Criminal Law Act 1977, S60, the Magistrates' Courts Act 1980, Sch 9, and the Criminal Justice Act 1982, s67)
Prosecution of Offences Act 1985: section 18
Criminal Justice Act 1982 – *A Guide to Fines* (1983). Butterworths.
Chandler, David (1987) *Fine Enforcement: Ideas from a Survey*, University of Cambridge Institute of Criminology. (Institute of Criminology occasional paper: No. 15).
Lomax, Ian S and Reynolds, Steven (1988) *Enforcement in the Magistrates' Court: a guide to enforcing money payments*, Fourmat.
Softley, Paul and Moxon, David (1982) *Fine Enforcement: an Evaluation of the Practices of Individual Courts.* Home Office Research and Planning Unit, Paper 12.
Home Office Circular 13/1984. *Fines and their Enforcement.*

Chapter 6: Probation Orders
Powers of Criminal Courts Act 1973: section 2 (as amended by the Criminal Law Act 1977, S57, Schs 12 and 13, SI 1978 No 474, and the Criminal Justice Act 1982, Schs 11 and 16); section 3 (as amended by the Mental Health Act 1983, Sch 4); section 4A (as inserted by the Criminal Justice Act 1982, Sch 11).

Chapter 7: Community Service Orders
Powers of Criminal Courts Act 1973: sections 14 and 15 (as amended by the Criminal Justice Act 1982, Schs 12 and 16 and the Criminal Law Act 1977, Sch 12)
Pease, K (1975) *Community Service Orders.* Home Office Research Study No. 29

Pease, K and others (1977) *Community Service Orders*. Home Office Research Study No. 39

Young, W (1979) *Community Service Orders*. Heinemann.

Reconviction of those given Community Service Orders (1983). Home Office Statistical Bulletin 18/83.

Home Office Circular 18/89 *National Standards for Community Service Orders*.

Chapter 8: Attendance Centre Orders

Criminal Justice Act 1982: sections 16 – 19.

Dunlop, Anne B (1980) *Junior Attendance Centres*, Home Office Research Study No. 60

Home Office Circular 42/83. *The Criminal Justice Act 1982 – implementation of Part I*.

Home Office Circular 22/86. *Attendance Centres*.

Home Office Circular 58/86. *Attendance Centres*.

Home Office Circular 59/87. *Attendance Centres*.

Chapter 9: Imprisonment

See chapters on the use of imprisonment in bibliography to Chapter 3 above.

Prison Statistics, England and Wales. Published annually, HMSO.

Report of the Work of the Prison Department. Published annually, HMSO.

Report of HM Chief Inspector of Prisons. Published annually, HMSO.

Report of the Parole Board. Published annually, HMSO.

Chapter 10: Custodial Penalties for Young Offenders

Criminal Justice Act 1982: sections 1 – 15 (as amended by the Criminal Justice Act 1988)

Criminal Justice Act, 1988: sections 123, 126, 130 and Schedule 8.

Children and Young Persons Act 1933: Section 53 (as amended by the Criminal Justice Act 1988 section 126).

Custodial sentences for young offenders; a discussion paper (1986) Home Office.

Chapter 11: Sentencing Juvenile Offenders

Criminal Justice Act 1982: sections 1 – 28.

Children and Young Persons Act 1933: Parts III and IV.

Children and Young Persons Act 1969: Part I (as amended by the Criminal Justice Act 1988 Schedule 10).

Bevan, H K (1989) *Child Law*, Butterworths.

Clarke, Hall and Morrison (10th edition 1985) *Law Relating to Children and Young Persons*, Butterworths (editors: Brian Harris and Richard White).

Moore, Terence G and Wilkinson, Tony P (1988) *The Juvenile Court: A Guide to Law and Practice*, Barry Rose.

Moxon, David, Jones, Peter and Tarling, Roger (1985) *Juvenile Sentencing: is there a tariff?* Home Office Research and Planning Unit, Paper 32.

Chapter 12: Mentally Disordered Offenders

Mental Health Act 1983, Part III in particular deals with the powers of the courts.

Mental Health Act 1983: Memorandum on Parts I – VI, VIII and X. Available from the Department of Health and Social Security.

Chapter 13: Disqualification from Driving

Road Traffic Offenders Act 1988 Sections 34 – 44

Butterworths handbook on the Road Traffic Act 1988, The Road Traffic Offenders Act 1988 and the Road Traffic (Consequential Provisions) Act 1988 (1989) Butterworths

Wilkinson's Road Traffic Law. (1987) Halnan and Wallis (eds), Oyez Longman.

Offences Relating to Motor Vehicles, England and Wales, Supplementary Tables 1987. Available from the Home Office.

Chapter 14: Recommendation for Deportation

Immigration Act 1971: section 3 – 6.

Immigration Act 1988: Paragraph 10 of the Schedule

Chapter 15: Ancillary Orders

Restitution – Criminal Justice Act 1972: section 6.

Forfeiture – Powers of Criminal Courts Act 1973: section 43.

Criminal Justice Act 1988 schedule 4.

Drug Trafficking Offences Act 1986.

Criminal Justice Act 1988

Criminal Justice Act 1988 (annotated by David Ashby) (1988) Shaw & Sons

Morton, James (1988) *The Criminal Justice Act 1987 and 1988: a commentary*, Waterloo.

Index

115

116

117

118

Printed in the U.K. for HMSO
Dd 292855 48186 6/90 C450